blues | LEGENDS

TO BILL AND JIM.

blues LEGENDS

CHARLES K. COWDERY

SALT LAKE CITY

First Edition

98 97 96 95   5 4 3 2 1

Copyright © 1995 by Charles K. Cowdery

This is a Peregrine Smith Book, published by
Gibbs Smith, Publisher
P.O. Box 667
Layton, Utah 84041

Design by Scott Van Kampen
Edited by Gail Yngve

Front cover photograph: Muddy Waters,
photographed by Raeburn Flerlage

Printed and bound in China

Library of Congress Cataloging-in-Publication Data

Cowdery, Chuck.
Blues legends/Chuck Cowdery.
p. cm.
ISBN 0-87905-688-6
Blues musicians--Biography. I. Title.
ML400.C68 1995
781.643'092'2—dc20
95-13142
[B] CIP
MN

CONTENTS

This amazing photograph was taken during a mid-1960s Howlin' Wolf performance at the legendary Silvio's Lounge on Chicago's West Side. Silvio's was a long-time blues staple and for many years was Howlin' Wolf's Chicago headquarters.

ABOUT THE IMAGES IN THIS BOOK

Most of the photographs in this book were taken by Raeburn Flerlage between approximately 1958 and 1972 in theaters, recording studios, blues clubs, hotel rooms, and homes in and around Chicago. In addition to being a photographer of blues performers, Flerlage has been a record distributor, music journalist, and radio disc jockey.

In 1944, Flerlage became the Midwest Secretary for People's Songs and worked with (but did not photograph) Pete Seeger, Woody Guthrie, and Leadbelly. The subject of his first professional photographs, in the late fifties, was blues piano legend Memphis Slim. For most of the next decade he photographed dozens if not hundreds of different blues artists, usually in performance, sometimes sitting for interviews, and sometimes just posing for his camera. Many of his photographs were taken for album covers, magazine articles and other publicity uses.

During the period when he was most active as a photographer, Flerlage shot Muddy Waters and Howlin' Wolf many times, in small clubs, in theaters, and in their homes. Virtually every other significant blues artist who played in Chicago during those years (and who didn't?) eventually came before his lens.

Some Flerlage images, individual shots from the famous Howlin' Wolf series at Silvios, for example, have been widely published. Many of the others reproduced here have never before or seldom been seen. Flerlage's photographs have never been collected to this extent and seldom reproduced this well.

Seen as a group, they give us a unique, in-depth picture of the Chicago blues scene during this dynamic period.

Born in 1915, the same year as Muddy Waters, Memphis Slim, Willie Dixon, and Robert Junior Lockwood, Ray Flerlage turned 80 in 1995. He lives on the South Side of Chicago with his wife, Luise.

Most of the advertising material reproduced in this book is from the Ralph Metcalfe Collection of the Chicago Blues Archives. Metcalfe was a blues promoter and manager, active primarily in the 1970s. The Chicago Blues Archives is housed at the Harold Washington Library Center of the Chicago Public Library.

Most of the records and album/CD covers reproduced in this book are from the collection of the author.

INTRODUCTION

Blues singer Bobby Bland works his magic on a 1960s Chicago audience.

"The blues had a child and they called it rock and roll." That is a simplified explanation of the relationship between these two musical forms, and it also describes the way most people today discover the blues—through its "child." Rock performers like Eric Clapton, the Rolling Stones, or ZZ Top play a blues classic or acknowledge their debt to the masters in an interview. Curious fans then go buy a Robert Johnson or Muddy Waters CD, or maybe something by Robert Cray or Stevie Ray Vaughn. They are surprised by how familiar the music sounds, even the Johnson recordings made in 1936–37.

Rolling Stones guitarist Keith Richards says that discovering Robert Johnson was "like a comet or a meteor that came along and, BOOM, suddenly he raised the ante, suddenly you just had to aim that much higher." Eric Clapton says that Johnson's singing "remains the most powerful cry that I think you can find in the human voice." In Memphis, the teenage Elvis Presley, sneaking into Beale Street blues clubs and theaters in the early fifties, absorbed the music of Arthur "Big Boy" Crudup and other local bluesmen. Presley's first hit single was Crudup's "That's All Right (Mama)."

THE MISUNDERSTOOD BLUES

The blues was, and is, much more than the midwife of rock and roll. It is a significant part of America's cultural heritage, especially the history of African-Americans. Though its roots go back to Africa, the blues is a truly American musical genre, influenced from the beginning by European-American culture and shaped by the experience of slavery and post-Reconstruction oppression in the rural South, particularly in the Mississippi River Delta.

There is, however, a problem with tying any music too closely to the culture that produced it. You risk discounting the individual creativity and personality of the artist. Reality gets distorted into an idealized myth. This has happened repeatedly with the blues. The most persistent myth is that most blues musicians are naive, unsophisticated "folk" artists instead of polished professional entertainers. White audiences, tired of the slick commercial music of Tin Pan Alley, sought authenticity and found it in the image of a poor farmer who laid down his plow at the end of the day and picked up a guitar.

When Big Bill Broonzy toured Europe in the early 1950s, he performed on acoustic guitar and was billed as a "black south-ern farmer" and the "last blues singer alive." In fact he had been making hit records in Chicago since 1926, and using electric instruments since the 1940s. When Broonzy died in 1958, many of his contemporaries, including chief guitar rival Lonnie Johnson, were very much alive and still performing. B. B. King is another example. Born and raised in Mississippi, he spent his early career working neither on a farm nor on the juke-joint circuit but in a radio station, first as a disc jockey and later as a performer. Even Robert Johnson, the most legendary bluesman of all, only picked cotton as a child. His entire short adult life was spent as a professional entertainer.

In fact virtually every blues artist whose name we know is a professional, trained and influenced by other professionals. They are men, and a few women, who diligently avoided manual labor of any kind. No dim country bumpkins, the earliest blues performers were the rebels and renegades of their communities. Blues was their ticket off the farm and into the wider world of travel, adventure, and good times. The informal but extensive African-American entertainment industry of which they were a part had already been in existence for several decades by the 1920s, when the first blues records were cut.

Early blues artists were worldly,

Mural over entrance to Chicago blues club Kingston Mines, April 1995.

describes it as "a folk song, passed back and forth between the races, that in truth was older than anyone's memory."

The West African roots of the blues rest primarily in the oral-history tradition of the griots, a caste of "living encyclopedias" who carried in their memories, and expressed through their songs, the collective knowledge of their tribe. When the New World slave trade began in the late fifteenth century, the griot tradition was already thousands of years old. Although this tradition was almost universal in West Africa, songs were specific to each tribe. Africans brought to America in slave ships came from dozens of cultures, scattered over a vast region. They spoke many languages and had different traditions. Certainly there were griots among these involuntary immigrants, but their songs could no longer serve their original purposes and soon were adapted to suit new circumstances.

In Africa, the griots always involved the whole community in their performances, with shouts, handclaps, stomping, and singing. In colonial America, their songs became the work tunes and "field hollers" that made the long, tedious hours of hard labor pass more easily. Singing was a natural way to make work more tolerable and was permitted by the overseers because it seemed to make the slaves more productive.

independent, and rebellious. Some commentators even hear, in early blues music, the first murmurs of the Civil Rights movement.

AMERICAN SYNTHESIS

Another persistent myth is that the blues is virtually a "pure African" music, uncontaminated by European-American influences until after World War II. In fact all African-American music, including the blues, incorporates European elements. The characteristic blues lyric, in which the second line of every verse repeats the first, comes from traditional Celtic ballads. Through its Celtic roots, the blues is also closely related to country music and influenced many early country stars like Jimmie Rodgers. If rock and roll is the child of the blues, then modern country music is at least its nephew.

Here is an example of how intertwined all of these musical sources really are. In 1955, Elvis Presley recorded "Mystery Train," a 1953 hit for Memphis bluesman Junior Parker. Although Parker (with producer Sam Phillips) is credited with writing the song, it is actually a traditional Celtic ballad recorded twenty years earlier, under a different name, by country music's famed Carter family. Greil Marcus, in his book *Mystery Train*,

Chicago's annual free Lakefront Blues Festival 1989 poster.

THE BIRTH OF THE BLUES

After the Civil War, field singing continued among the freed slaves, most of whom became sharecroppers. Soon variations on the old songs were also being performed by traveling musicians at picnics, dances, juke joints, and country suppers. The audience still participated, but now the griot had a guitar. This was the birth of the blues.

In addition to the Delta blues of Mississippi and Arkansas, other strains evolved independently in the Southeast and Southwest. When blacks began to leave the region in large numbers after 1900, they took their music to new homes in the cities of the North and West. Most migrants from the Delta went north to Chicago, Detroit, and other industrial cities of the Midwest. From Texas, Oklahoma, and Louisiana, they went west to California. Eastern bluesmen either stayed in the region or moved to New York.

In 1943, in the last great wave of the African-American exodus, twenty-eight-year-old Muddy Waters left the Stovall Plantation in Mississippi, headed for Chicago.

In 1944, he was given his first electric guitar by an uncle. In 1946, he started recording. The electric blues was born, and rock and roll became inevitable.

WHITE AMERICA DISCOVERS THE BLUES

For most of the twentieth century, blues was the most popular music among African-Americans, but it remained largely unknown to white audiences. During the 1930s, Alan Lomax and his father, John, recorded many blues musicians for the Library of Congress, and Leadbelly began to perform in Greenwich Village coffeehouses alongside Pete Seeger and Woody Guthrie, but these voices were rarely heard in the European-American heartland. After World War II, white Americans in larger numbers slowly began to discover the blues through radio and records. When rock and rollers began to mine the blues for material, more young, middle-class, white listeners became curious. Most of the blues songs they heard were still "covers" by white performers, but a few blues-infused blacks like Chuck Berry, Fats Domino, and Bo Diddley were starting to break through.

Meanwhile, in postwar Europe, the successful tours of Big Bill Broonzy were followed by a multiple-artist show called the American Folk Blues Festival, which featured Muddy Waters, Willie Dixon, T-Bone Walker, John Lee Hooker, and other electric blues innovators. These performances, plus blues records on Sam Phillips's Sun label, reached the ears of fledgling English rock musicians like Eric Clapton, Keith Richards, John Lennon, Jimmy Page, Jeff Beck, Peter Green, and many others. These young, white Englishmen embraced the Chicago-style electric blues with passionate enthusiasm. They called themselves bluesmen, called their groups blues bands, and paid homage to their idols. The Yardbirds, Fleetwood Mac, Cream, the Rolling Stones, Led Zeppelin, and many other groups started out as electric blues bands. At their first U.S. press conference, the Beatles were asked what they most wanted to see in America; they replied, "Muddy Waters and Bo Diddley." The American reporter's follow-up question was "Where's that?"

Back in the United States, the folk revival of the early 1960s introduced new white audiences to the acoustic blues of artists like Leadbelly (who had died in 1949), Son House, Mississippi John Hurt, and Bukka White. This audience existed mostly in big cities and on university campuses. Artists like Willie Dixon, John Lee Hooker and Muddy Waters, all of whom had been playing electric blues for nearly twenty years, picked up acoustic instruments again to capitalize on the new fad. Later in the decade, the influence and tremendous success of the British bands led to the founding of several white American electric-blues bands (Paul Butterfield, Mike Bloomfield, the Allman Brothers, Canned Heat, Johnny Winter) and a belated discovery of the music of Waters, Dixon, Hooker, Howlin' Wolf, Lightnin' Hopkins, and others.

During this same period, black audiences outside the rural South (the ones with money to spend on records and in nightclubs) began to reject the blues. They considered it too old-fashioned and unsophisticated. Even the electric blues was too "country" for most members of the new, emerging, black middle class. The blues reminded them of times and places they were glad to forget. They preferred rhythm and blues, soul, and modern jazz. When the white audience's interest also began to wane in the 1970s, the blues fell on hard times.

THE RIGHT-NOW BLUES

Finally, in the 1980s, Chicago officialdom realized the tourism value of a thriving blues scene and started to encourage and promote it. The popularity of films like *The Blues Brothers* made a trip to a blues club a must for every Chicago visitor. Today the Chicago blues has been institutionalized as part of the city's official self-image, most notably through the annual Chicago Blues Festival. You can still hear country blues in small towns throughout the Delta, and the Texas blues is alive and well in Austin. Although some people worry that the music will lose its vitality and become a historical curiosity, like Dixieland jazz in New Orleans, at least now there is little chance that the blues will ever disappear entirely.

PROFILES

The selection of artists for this book is not intended to reflect a judgment about their importance, relative either to each other or to other artists not profiled here. Rather, the intent is to offer a sampling of musicians representing different eras and styles, from the first blues recordings in the 1920s up to the present.

Blues fans in Chicago, circa 1965.

BLIND LEMON JEFFERSON

The two men were born, lived and died a decade apart. They began life five hundred miles from each other, both in cotton country, and both traveled widely. They died young and have been lionized by subsequent generations as preeminent practitioners of their art form, the country blues. There the similarities end. The younger man was thin and handsome. The older man was fat, almost constantly drunk, and blind since birth.

Did Blind Lemon Jefferson and Robert Johnson ever meet? It is something to ponder, since both men have been called "the father of rock and roll." Is it possible? Robert Johnson, who turned eighteen in the last year of Jefferson's life, just might have seen the older man perform. He undoubtedly knew Jefferson's recordings and would have jumped at the opportunity to see him if Jefferson had come to town. Johnson, however, would not have had much to contribute musically. He was just a mannish boy then, beginning his blues journey. Blind Lemon Jefferson was a star.

When the music of both men was rediscovered in the 1960s, Johnson became the favorite of English blues rockers, while Jefferson was adopted by American folk rockers. Jefferson's legend had been part of the American folk-music tradition since Leadbelly had taught some of his songs to Pete Seeger and Woody Guthrie in the 1930s. He is the "Jefferson" in Jefferson Airplane. His "Matchbox," a hit in 1927, has been rerecorded by everyone from Jerry Lee Lewis and Carl Perkins to the Beatles. His "Corrina Blues" has been interpreted by everyone from Bob Dylan to Chet Atkins.

By the mid-1920s, phonographs had become so inexpensive that even poor sharecroppers could afford them. Jefferson's songs were the first large body of true, unadulterated country blues to be recorded and commercially

BLIND LEMON JEFFERSON

King of the Country Blues
First in-depth documentary of
Blind Lemon Jefferson and his music

Cordially Yours
Blind Lemon Jefferson

distributed to this wide audience, beginning in 1926. For many black families, especially in the rural areas, a record by Blind Lemon Jefferson was the first one they ever bought. Jefferson became the first country-blues recording star. After 1926, several generations of young, aspiring blues guitarists learned how to play by copying Blind Lemon Jefferson records.

Born in 1897 on a farm about sixty miles southeast of Dallas, Lemon was the youngest of nine children. "Lemon" was his real first name, not a nickname. Though he was born blind, it never kept him from playing with the other children, even when they tore off across the fields. Somehow he always managed to keep up.

As a blind man, Jefferson had few career options in a poor farming community. Music and the ministry were about it. Although he did try some preaching, music seemed to suit him

This is the only known picture of Blind Lemon Jefferson, used by his record company in their advertising.

best, and he began his career at age fourteen. Every day he would walk into Wortham, the nearest town, and sit down in front of the feed store or the dry goods emporium to play and sing for tips. His family wired a tin cup to the neck of his guitar, and he learned how to identify the denomination of a coin deposited there by the sound it made hitting the tin. As his popularity grew, he was invited to play at country picnics in the area, some of which drew hundreds of people.

Even as a boy, Jefferson's large body produced a powerful, agile, and expressive voice. His large size may also have made him less vulnerable to thieves as he traveled the familiar, but sometimes hazardous, country roads alone. His size and toughness led as well to his only known job outside of music, as a professional wrestler.

At about the age of twenty, Lemon Jefferson was ready to see what the big city could offer him, so he headed for Dallas. For a black musician, Dallas meant "Deep Ellum," the only place where he was likely to find work, playing for black laborers and white cowboys in brothels and taverns. On a typical night, he would set up in a suitable brothel with another musician or two and begin to play, a bottle of whiskey within reach. He usually spent most of his share the same night on whiskey and sex, but somehow accumulated enough cash over the next few years to obtain a car and driver, with which he made a triumphant visit home.

During his days in Dallas, and in the other towns he visited, Jefferson was a street musician just as he had been back in Wortham. So he could change location frequently, it was his custom to retain a local youth as his "lead boy." Lightnin' Hopkins and T-Bone Walker both served in this capacity.

Jefferson made his first recordings in Chicago in early 1925, but the record company, Paramount, did not release them right away. They brought him back for another session in 1926 and released these sides first. The record was a hit, as were most of its successors until 1928. Jefferson made about eighty records in all.

By 1929, Chicago was as much Jefferson's home as anyplace else. He probably was about thirty-two years old, but may have been as old as forty-nine, according to some accounts. He was still making money, even though his career was fading, and he continued to live a hard life of nonstop music and partying that ended on most nights in a drunken stupor. After one such party on a snowy night in December, Blind Lemon Jefferson died. In one story, he got lost in a blizzard and froze to death; in another story he had a heart attack; a third story relates it was a heart attack, but he was in his car and the driver dumped his body into the gutter; still another has it that a jealous woman poisoned his coffee.

When news of Jefferson's death spread to his fans around the country, many were deeply saddened. To help ease their pain, his record company released several "tribute" records, including at least one sermon. In his eulogy, Reverend Emmet Dickenson compared Jefferson to another famous figure, but it wasn't Robert Johnson. It was Jesus Christ: "Like Him, unto the age of thirty, he was unknown, and also like Him, in the space of a little over three years, this man and his works were in every home."

It would be impossible to list all of the bluesmen who were influenced by Blind Lemon Jefferson, but they include Lightnin' Hopkins, T-Bone Walker, B. B. King, Big Bill Broonzy, Muddy Waters, John Lee Hooker, Buddy Guy, Howlin' Wolf, and Big Joe Williams. Jefferson is also cited as an influence on musicians as diverse as Louis Armstrong and Chet Atkins.

Blind Lemon Jefferson was the product of a tradition already many generations old when he came along, but people heard about it all for the first time from him. For us in the audience, for whom recordings are the only way of knowing what this music sounded like in its earliest form, Blind Lemon Jefferson is where the blues begins.

MEMPHIS MINNIE

The blues tradition that most influenced modern popular music is that of the self-accompanied singer/songwriter. This tradition of the traveling musician who sings and plays guitar, and whose original songs address current events as well as timeless themes, is the "country blues" that begot the "urban blues" that begot rock and roll. These musicians have been almost exclusively male. Lizzie "Memphis Minnie" Douglas is the rare exception.

The singers usually named as the great blueswomen—Bessie Smith, Ma Rainey, Sippie Wallace, Victoria Spivey, and many others—are from a different tradition, usually called "classic blues." This strain was born in the popular theater of the early twentieth

Record company publicity photograph, 1930s.

century known as vaudeville. It combined blues ideas with then-popular European-American song forms to produce a sophisticated, sexy sound recognizable as the blues, but also different.

"Classic" makes it sound old, but it was actually the newest thing, created by the first generation of African-American musicians to penetrate the mainstream of the American entertainment industry. Exemplified by Bessie Smith and W.C. Handy, they were professional musicians, often well trained in the musical idioms of the dominant white culture. They generally had not "lived" the blues except peripherally. The term "classic" applies because this

was the first type of blues to be recorded, beginning in 1921, and remained virtually the only style of blues recorded until the end of that decade.

There is sometimes a tendency to portray the classic tradition as female and the country tradition as male, but this is not accurate. The purveyors of classic blues were both men and women. Its composers and musicians were mostly men, while the singers were mostly women. Country blues, the American griot tradition of the traveling, self-accompanied singer/songwriter, consisted almost entirely of men. Almost, but not entirely.

Memphis Minnie was not the

only women "in the blues," but their numbers were small, and she was unquestionably the most successful. For more than twenty years, she was among a handful of top blues performers, one of the few who survived the Depression with her career largely intact. She wrote most of the songs she performed, was an early innovator on both National steel and electric guitars, and was the clear leader of the various ensembles in which she worked. The groups always included her man of the moment, and often other musicians as well.

Why did so few women follow the life Memphis Minnie chose? The answer lies in the sexual mores of the time. In the nineteenth and early twentieth centuries, show business was not considered a respectable occupation for anyone, male or female, white or black. The main reason for this social disapproval was the fact that popular entertainers, especially singers, invariably traded on whatever sex appeal they had. Advertising their sexual availability, whether actual or symbolic, was part of their act. Across cultures, this is probably the most universal theme in popular music, and while it invariably conflicts with society's official attitudes about some sexual behavior, it usually reinforces having different standards for men and women.

In African-American culture, the

taboo against women playing the blues was so strong it was almost completely successful. Women could sing sacred songs in church or at home, but they could not sing the blues in barrelhouses. A woman who violated this taboo could not be a member of the church and was, therefore, cut off from the support of the female community. Sure, male blues performers were considered the spawn of the devil, too, but a woman who played guitar and sang the blues in public was also assumed to be a whore, a lash of social censure for which there is no masculine equivalent. Memphis Minnie did not avoid these assumptions or that censure; she simply disregarded them and succeeded in spite of them.

Although classic blues artists like Bessie Smith suffered the same social disapproval, their situation was more tolerable

MEMPHIS MINNIE

because they typically performed in theaters, insulated from the audience. Minnie played in bars and dance halls, where the heady mixture of alcohol, gambling, and sex was always present. She performed on the dance floor or on a makeshift platform. There was no orchestra pit, no backstage dressing room. She was right there, unprotected.

Playing the blues in the kinds of places where blues was played was dangerous for musicians of both sexes. Robert Johnson was only the best-known victim of his own successful sexual advertising. Jealous boyfriends and husbands, as well as jilted lovers, ended the lives of many bluesmen. For a woman, the obvious additional risk was sexual assault.

Memphis Minnie's solution was twofold. She always traveled and performed with a male partner, a husband for most of her career, but she also developed a reputation as a very rough customer. Minnie could take care of herself and made sure everyone knew it. She was quick with a bottle or a knife, and she didn't play an all-steel National guitar just for its sound. In Chicago, word was that she had killed more than one man back in Mississippi. Minnie laid down her rules so swiftly, decisively, and forcefully that there was no excuse for ignorance: Look all you want and listen, please, but touch without being asked, and you will lose

something; make no mistake.

Memphis Minnie began life as Lizzie Douglas in Algiers, Louisiana, in 1897. She was the oldest of thirteen children and was always "Kid" to her family, never Lizzie. "Memphis Minnie" was a name she was given much later by a white record-company executive.

When "Kid" Douglas was seven, her family moved north to Walls, Mississippi, a small town just south of Memphis, Tennessee. About a year later, Douglas got her first guitar. She would do anything to avoid farm work, including run off to Memphis and play for nickels in the parks around Beale Street. During World War I, she toured the South with the Ringling Brothers traveling show out of Clarksdale, Mississippi.

Toward the end of her run with the circus, while in her late teens or early twenties, Kid Douglas began to follow the blues in her own particular way. She would hook up with a man as lover, protector, and musical partner. He would play rhythm guitar to her lead, and both would sing and contribute songs. For about ten years, Douglas auditioned men for this job, including Willie Brown, who also worked with Robert Johnson and Son House.

During this period, just after World War I, Kid Douglas was one of the few black entertainers hired to play at parties for the white aristocracy of the area, usually when

W.C. Handy was not available. She knew how to satisfy these audiences because of her traveling-show experience, and she used that income to supplement the meager amounts she made playing blues.

Around the time she turned thirty, Kid Douglas hooked up with Joe McCoy. In 1929, the couple cut their first six sides in New York for Columbia, including one of their biggest hits, "Bumble Bee Blues." When the first sides from that session were released, the couple became "Kansas Joe and Memphis Minnie." Although her new name was coined by the record company, it suited her. Lizzie Douglas was no longer a kid. She was Memphis Minnie McCoy, popular blues recording artist.

Like most blues singers, Minnie's whole life was spent on the road, whether recording in New York or Chicago, or touring the Midwest and South. Memphis was her home as much as any other place, but she also lived in Jackson, Mississippi, the state capital, where Joe McCoy had been raised. After the success of their early records, Minnie and Joe McCoy moved their base of operations to Chicago, but they returned to the South often.

Unlike many blues artists, the recording career of Kansas Joe and Memphis Minnie survived the Depression, although it was greatly diminished. Retail prices

for their records fell from seventy-five to thirty-five cents or less, and times were tough financially. There were personal and artistic differences, too. As their careers matured, it became clear that Minnie was the star of the pair, a fact that did not sit well with Kansas Joe. They split in 1935.

Minnie was now a major star in the stable of Lester Melrose, who produced virtually all of the blues recordings made in the United States between 1934 and 1951, most of them with the same core group of musicians. The Melrose group included Memphis Minnie, Big Bill Broonzy, Tampa Red, Arthur "Big Boy" Crudup, Lonnie Johnson, Roosevelt Sykes, and many others. By 1939, Minnie had hooked up with Ernest "Little Son Joe" Lawlars, who was her partner for the rest of her career.

During the 1930s, Minnie's guitar style gradually evolved. She developed, along with Tampa Red and Lonnie Johnson, a single-string picking style that characterized what came to be called the "urban blues." Their innovations inspired T-Bone Walker and B. B. King and can be heard today in the playing of virtually every guitarist born since 1950. Minnie was also one of the first to play in this new style on an electric guitar. She had already helped change the fundamental sound of blues guitar once before, when she was among the first to use a National

steel. Later, in the 1950s, she was one of the first blues guitarists to play standing up, a seemingly minor change in performing style but one that was universally adopted thereafter.

Memphis Minnie enjoyed her greatest commercial success during the 1940s. She and Lawlars recorded a string of hits, including "Me and My Chauffeur Blues," her biggest. Like her earlier hit, "Bumble Bee Blues," it was sexual advertisement at its most explicit, as frankly erotic as any blues recorded by a male singer of the period. In no uncertain terms, Minnie told her listeners what she wanted and why: "Wants to see

★ ★

my chauffeur, wants to see my chauffeur, I wants him to drive me, I wants him to drive me—downtown." (A little guitar riff.) "Says he drives so easy, I can't turn him down." Minnie still sang with a full country twang after more than twenty years off the farm, which added to her earthy appeal.

Throughout the 1940s and well into the 1950s, Minnie and Lawlars were in demand at all of the top Chicago clubs, including The Gate, a popular West Side tavern operated by Ruby Lee Gatewood. The Gate was the site of Memphis Minnie's famous weekly "Blue Monday" parties, but her main club base was the 708 on the South Side.

In her midforties, Minnie Lawlars continued to enhance her lifelong reputation for hard living. Her fellow musicians, all men, remember her as drinking, cursing, gambling, fighting, chewing tobacco, and playing guitar "just like a man." Her fans, both male and female, regularly awarded her the prizes in "cutting" contests against other guitarists.

Although her career declined in the 1950s, Minnie still had many fans, but by the time Big Bill Broonzy died in 1958, the party was just about over for the Lawlarses as well. Their lifestyle had taken its toll on both of them. Son Joe had a serious heart condition that prevented him from performing, so he and Minnie moved back to Memphis.

Record company publicity photograph, 1940s.

For Minnie, the party had lasted more than forty years. When she began to have circulatory problems of her own, they moved in with her youngest sister. Joe died in 1961, and Minnie continued her slow decline for the next twelve years. She had no money and received no royalties for the many songs she had written and recorded. Donations from fans paid for a few comforts near the end. She died in 1973.

Memphis Minnie's career was full of singular accomplishments, the greatest of which was the sum of them all. She was literally the only woman of her time to accomplish what she did, and she overcame enormous obstacles to do it. Memphis Minnie's legacy is that she did exactly as she pleased.

BIG JOE WILLIAMS

Big Joe Williams was one of the few Delta bluesmen of his generation (he was born in 1903) who performed and recorded abundantly on both sides of World War II, who roamed and sang almost continuously for six decades, and who never strayed from his country roots.

Big Joe Williams was a rarity among blues artists in another way as well. Credited as the writer of the blues standard, "Baby, Please Don't Go," he fought for and actually received some of his composer's royalties. That small windfall toward the end of his life helped him buy a house in rural eastern Mississippi,

Performing in the mid-1960s with a very young Mike Bloomfield on bass.

about fifteen miles from the cabin in Knoxford Swamp where he had been born and raised.

Williams began his career with the simple goal of most bluesmen: to get off the farm. He knew at an early age that he did not want to plow or chop cotton. His first musical instrument was a one-string guitar he made from a board, a wire, and two nails. His mother and father were both musicians and taught him many songs.

As a teenager, Williams avoided farm work by hiring out as a contract laborer on large construction projects, usually building or repairing railroad beds or the system of levees along the Mississippi River. This turned out to be a case of leaping out of the frying pan into the fire. Like the sharecropper system, the contract-labor system was slavery in fact if not name. Just as the sharecropper was always in debt to the plantation

Big Joe Williams on the front steps of his Chicago home in the early 1960s, with his famous nine-string guitar. Note the three extra tuning pegs at the top.

owner, so the contract laborer was always in debt to the contractor.

The men were paid low wages, then charged "on account" for room, board, even Saturday-night parties complete with whiskey and prostitutes. Few men got ahead in this game, and most became permanently bound to the contractor. They either continued to work for nothing or ran away.

The workday on a contract gang was long and brutal, and the brutality continued after dark in the camps. Bosses exercised absolute con-

trol by frequently demonstrating their capacity for sudden and intense cruelty. Every day the boss made sure his employees understood that their lives meant nothing, less than the life of a mule, and could be ended by him on a whim.

Joe Williams was a big man, strong and tough, able to survive in this world. A good laborer, he also entertained in the camps and always knew when to push on. When he drifted back home to Crawford, picnics and dances put a few dollars in his pocket. From there, he might head over to Tuscaloosa, Alabama, the nearest big town, where he could work for the local black vice boss. Williams at this time was a young man in his late teens and early twenties, indulging every appetite. As he flirted with women, he alerted their men in his lyrics: "If that's your woman, you better put her to your side, 'cause if she flag my train, I'm sure going to let her ride."

When he wasn't traveling alone, Williams roamed with a medicine show or minstrel troupe. He did this throughout the 1920s. When the Depression began, people no longer had as much money to spend on entertainment so he went back to contract labor. He also tried big-city life, moving to St. Louis to live with a cousin.

From childhood on, Williams constructed, repaired, and modified his instruments. The modifi-

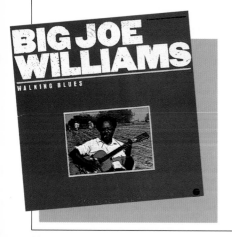

cation that became his trademark was the nine-string guitar. By doubling up the three bass strings, he got more volume, strumming them with his thumb to create the beat while picking out lead runs with his fingers. To intensify the rhythmic effect even more, he attached metal objects to his guitar, like cans and pie plates, that would rattle and buzz as he played. His contemporary, Son House, achieved similar results by adopting the National steel guitar as his principal instrument.

From 1935 until the beginning of World War II, Big Joe Williams (then known as "Po Jo" Williams) recorded on the Bluebird label for Lester Melrose. Though officially part of the Melrose group, Williams never adopted the urban blues sound or the lifestyle of his contemporaries, Big Bill Broonzy and Tampa Red. He was hired as a country-blues singer, and he remained that through dozens of successful releases. On some of his most successful Bluebird sides, Williams was paired with a young harmonica virtuoso, John Lee "Sonny Boy" Williamson. The sounds they created were a preview of what Muddy Waters and Little Walter were going to achieve fifteen years later.

In 1935, Williams made the first of his many recordings of "Baby, Please Don't Go." He was listed then and thereafter as the song's composer, and though it was

probably a traditional blues tune, he claimed it, became associated with it, and ultimately made a little money from it when the song was recorded and rerecorded countless times in blues, rhythm-and-blues, and rock versions.

Throughout his life, Williams was always traveling. When he finished recording in Chicago, he might stay around for a few days, but usually he went back on the road, returning to either St. Louis or Mississippi by some circuitous route. Along the way, he might hook up with other bluesmen to travel and perform together. He worked with Muddy Waters in Mississippi shortly before he moved to Chicago. He also worked with Robert Johnson for a brief time in St. Louis.

After the war, not much changed for Big Joe Williams. He continued to travel the country, recording country blues for a host of different companies and playing his blues for people along the way. He didn't electrify; he didn't hire a drummer. He might work with another guitar or a harp player, but that was about it. When the blues revival began, he made the switch from black to white audiences, but nothing else changed. His performance for an audience of two thousand in a European concert hall was identical to his performance for an audience of twenty at a country picnic. Intense and personal, ragged and raw, it was the

country blues and nothing else.

Big Joe Williams recorded a number of albums in the sixties and seventies in this same uncompromising style. He was a regular on the blues-festival circuit in the U.S. and Europe, and never really stopped roaming until he was in his late seventies. He died in 1982 at the age of seventy-nine.

Big Joe Williams had the scarred face of a man who lived his blues.

SON HOUSE

Before there was Muddy Waters or Robert Johnson, there was Son House. For the first forty-six of his eighty-six years, he was the Delta bluesman incarnate, the reality behind the stereotype. During his second musical career, in the 1960s, House spoke with sweetness but still sang with the rage of a man born and raised African-American in "Jim Crow" Mississippi, where senseless brutality and humiliation were part of his daily life.

As both a songwriter and performer, Son House was an

The body of a National guitar was assembled from pieces of sheet steel. The design made the guitar louder but also gave it a buzzing, metallic sound, preferred by Son House and others.

enormous influence on the generation of bluesmen that followed him, the ones who brought the music north and eventually carried it around the world. Son House taught Muddy Waters directly and influenced many other artists of that generation, particularly Johnson, Albert King, and Eddie Taylor.

Son House was born Eddie James House, Jr., in 1902 on a plantation near the town of Lyon in Coahoma County, Mississippi. When he was still very young, his parents separated, and House moved to Louisiana with his mother to work in the cotton fields. There he heard the hollers

SON HOUSE

From Yazoo Records Heroes of the Blues cards, illustrated by R. Crumb.

Son House posing for publicity stills, 1964.

he believed were the basis of the blues. "When I was a boy, we always was singing in the fields," he recalled. "Not real singing, you know, just hollering. But we made up our songs about things that was happening to us at the time, and I think that's where the blues started."

With his mother, House was an avid churchgoer and grew up singing sacred music, which should have precluded a blues career, according to the moral proscriptions of his day. At age fifteen he started preaching. For the next decade or so, the church was his true calling, and he eventually pastored a Baptist congregation in his hometown of Lyon, Mississippi. He also worked for a time at a steel mill in East St. Louis, Illinois.

In the mid-1920s, House began playing blues guitar at dances, parties, and picnics. The spiritual conflict for him must have been enormous. *His* people--church people--believed that the blues was Satan's music. Stringed, lute-type instruments like the guitar were especially evil, "the devil's own riding horses." Thirty years later, white suburban parents and preachers would make similar declarations about rock and roll.

In the song "Preachin' Blues," House gives his own ironic explanation for the path he chose. "Oh, I had religion, Lord, to this very day," he sings. "But the women and whiskey, well, they would not let me pray."

Son House learned to play slide

Son House performing, 1964.

guitar from an otherwise-unknown Clarksdale guitarist named Lemon, who took his repertoire from Blind Lemon Jefferson's recordings. Although Jefferson was a Texan, he recorded more than eighty songs for the Paramount label in the mid- to late-1920s, and his music was well known in the Delta. We have an image of Delta life as very primitive, and in most ways it was, but some modern conveniences did exist, and the phonograph was one of them. Consequently, a number of record companies created "race" categories to supply African-American phonograph owners with music. Blind Lemon Jefferson was one of the stars.

Another Paramount star was Charlie Patton, a local Delta man. House was about twenty-six when he first hooked up with Patton, playing parties and picnics with him and fiddler Willie Brown (the same "friend-boy Willie Brown" mentioned in Robert Johnson's "Cross Road Blues"). Not long after these first collaborations, House got into a fight at a house party near Lyon. Pistols were drawn and fired. When the smoke cleared, House was standing, the other man was dead. House pleaded self-defense but was convicted of murder and sent to the Mississippi state farm at

Parchman, where he served two years. The judge who paroled him suggested he leave the area, advice House did not hesitate to take.

Soon after his release, House joined Patton and Brown to record some sides for Paramount at a studio in Grafton, Wisconsin. For himself, House recorded "My Black Mama," "Preachin' Blues" and "Dry Spell Blues." He apparently was paid a flat fifteen dollars for each song he recorded. This was typical compensation at the time for artists on "race" labels. They received a flat session fee and no royalties for either their performances or their original songs.

Though he may have stayed away from Lyon, House returned to the Delta after the 1930 recording sessions and continued to work with Patton until the older man died four years later. He also maintained a relationship with Willie Brown, both in and out of music, for the next twenty years.

In 1942, researcher Alan Lomax was almost arrested because he referred to House, a black man, as "Mister House" in a conversation with the Tunica County sheriff. Tunica is the next county north of Coahoma, and Lomax was there recording House and three other musicians in a local barrelhouse when the session was interrupted by the plantation boss, for whom House worked as a tractor driver. The boss later marched Lomax off to the sheriff, who effectively ran him out of town for being a suspected "outside agitator." One of the songs recorded at that session and released by the Library of Congress was "Death Letter Blues," one of House's best-known compositions. Not long after the incident with Lomax, House and Willie Brown abandoned the Delta and moved to Rochester, New York, where they performed occasionally until Brown returned to Tunica, where he died in 1952. During the 1940s and 1950s, House worked in manufacturing and as a railroad porter. In 1964, he was "rediscovered" by white blues fans and promoters, who urged him to start performing again. From then until 1971, he played dozens of festival and club dates in the United States and Europe, and made several powerful new recordings. Not only did his second career expose House and his music to a much wider audience, but it also gave the next generation of blues artists a chance to get to know him as a man as well as a musician. Buddy Guy was one such admirer, who would smuggle whiskey to House before the old man went onstage at big festivals. Once berated for it by promoter Dick Waterman, Guy exclaimed, "Don't stop Son House from having his fun. Just let him have his two or three drinks and his fifteen or twenty minutes, how long it takes him to get high, 'cause you can't redo him at eighty-five." (House was actually about sixty-five at the time.)

Son House rarely performed in public after 1971. His health wasn't good, but he lived another seventeen years, dying in Detroit in 1988 at age eighty-six. Son House is in the line of artists—along with Blind Lemon Jefferson, Robert Johnson, and Muddy Waters—who most inspired later rock guitarists from the Rolling Stones to Jefferson Airplane (who chose "Jefferson" in tribute to Blind Lemon). Unlike Jefferson, Johnson, and many, many others, House was able to realize at least some rewards and recognition for his contribution, albeit late in his life.

ARTHUR "BIG BOY" CRUDUP

In the segregated South, folk music made by blacks was called blues, while folk music created by whites was called hillbilly. Both kinds of music were recorded by companies up north, which categorized and sold them back to their respective constituencies down south. Blues and hillbilly music used most of the same instruments and had almost the same roots. They were never that different. It was mostly the skin color of the musicians that kept them apart.

Actually the blues had the exact same roots as hillbilly music, and African elements that whites rarely heard. Since slavery, the best African-American musicians knew how to play the music whites liked, so they could enter-

Arthur Crudup recording session, late 1960s.

tain at white events. These influences were incorporated into the blues throughout its development. Since white musicians never had occasion to play in a black barrelhouse, they had no reason to learn black music.

In 1954, that particular racial barrier was breached, and something was created that changed popular music all over the world. A white, nineteen-year-old truck driver named Elvis Presley recorded a song that had been written and recorded eight years earlier by a black farmer/bluesman named Arthur Crudup. White singers had recorded songs written by blacks before, even blues, but the new wrinkle this time was that the white man sang and played the song exactly like the black man, phrase for phrase, change for change.

Presley never denied it. He told

interviewers the way it was done, how his music was born: "Down in Tupelo, Mississippi, I used to hear old Arthur Crudup bang his box the way I do now, and I said if I ever got to the place I could feel what old Arthur felt, I'd be a music man like nobody ever

saw." The song Presley recorded in 1954, "That's All Right," launched his career, but it never did much for Crudup.

Arthur Crudup (pronounced CROOD-up) was born in 1905 on a Mississippi farm. He was dubbed "Big Boy" in childhood for all the usual reasons. As a man, he became a sharecropper like his parents and never thought about becoming a bluesman until he was almost thirty.

After learning the guitar and spending a few years working in Mississippi juke joints, he headed for Chicago in 1940 with a gospel quartet and stayed behind with a girlfriend. The girlfriend's aunt, who also lived in the house, soon threw him out. Left without any other options, he sold his blues on South Side street corners and slept in a cardboard box.

One day a peripheral member of the musical community around producer Lester Melrose heard Crudup on the street. He put a small donation into Crudup's hat and told the singer to stay put, returning a little while later with Melrose. Crudup was auditioned and accepted by the other musicians, but Melrose made it clear he wanted original songs. Crudup had been singing standard blues and current blues hits, improvising lyrics like everyone else did, but not really writing.

By 1942, he had adapted. Not only did he record original songs, but he accompanied himself on electric guitar with a washtub bass behind him. Crudup was a very limited guitar player. He only knew three chords. The electric instrument helped. It also complemented his voice, which had a high, ringing quality with the clear, forceful tone of a mule skinner's shout. Behind Crudup's very country voice, Melrose put an electric guitar, bass, and drums. The songs were simple but effective, and Crudup developed a knack for the fundamentals of pop songwriting: simple hooks, reliable boy/girl themes, and lots of repetition.

But Big Boy Crudup was frustrated in a big way. Records that sold well were supposed to pay royalties, and Crudup wasn't receiving any, even when his songs were hits. The session fees all the musicians received for recording weren't enough to live on, but all the rest of the Melrose group supported themselves by playing in Chicago nightspots and touring. Records made them more marketable, so they put up with being robbed. Crudup couldn't do that because he had bad stage fright. Between recording sessions in Chicago, he went back to his farm in Mississippi. In 1952, he quit in disgust. Although he continued to record from time to time, he never worked for Melrose again.

When Presley's "That's All Right" became a hit in 1954, Crudup started asking about his royalties again. Melrose said he would look into it but nothing happened. All during the rock era, "That's All Right" and other Crudup songs were recorded by artists like Creedence Clearwater Revival, Elton John, Rod Stewart, Johnny Winter, Paul Butterfield, Buffy Saint-Marie, Tina Turner, Canned Heat, and B. B. King. Crudup was always credited on the records, and the royalties were paid to the publishing company, but nothing ever came to him.

In the late 1960s, Dick Waterman took over Arthur Crudup's management. Waterman also managed the careers of several other blues artists, including Buddy Guy, mostly booking them into bars and festivals where the audience was predominantly white. Strangely, Crudup was no longer afraid to play in front of an audience and managed to earn a little money.

Starting in 1968, Waterman also tried to get Crudup his back royalties, working through the American Guild of Authors and Composers (AGAC). The guild's lawyers negotiated with the publishing company's lawyers, and in 1971, they thought they had a deal firm enough to bring Crudup and his four children to New York to sign all the papers and receive a check for sixty thousand dollars.

BIG BOY CRUDUP

Crudup was sixty-six years old at the time and living a hand-to-mouth existence in Virginia. That money would have assured him a comfortable retirement. At the last minute, the publisher rejected the deal. Crudup died three years later, broke.

Crudup is primarily remembered because of "That's All Right" and the subsequent royalties' dispute, but much of his other music is also worth hearing, especially the other Melrose-produced sides made between 1946 and 1952. These tracks combine country blues, Chicago blues, hillbilly music, and then-current popular song styles in new ways. When Elvis Presley and Sam Phillips heard Crudup, they both knew about all of these other music styles, too, and they felt this was something different, something new, something that would sell. They were right.

ROOSEVELT SYKES

The music that spawned the blues, the work songs and field hollers of the Mississippi Delta, was generally sung unaccompanied. The first instruments married to the blues were the guitar and harmonica. Simple, portable, and cheap, they were the perfect instruments for poor agricultural workers seeking careers as traveling musicians.

The piano came later, when bluesmen arrived in the cities and discovered that an upright piano, properly pounded, could make one man sound like a whole band. This was good, because partners had to be paid and musicians could always make more money on

At the piano, 1970.

their own. All they had to do was keep a big, noisy, crowded room dancing happily. Steel-bodied guitars were one way of raising the volume in those days before amplification. The piano, when one could be found, was another.

The earliest blues piano arrangements were probably straight transpositions from the guitar, but the percussive potential of the piano was irresistible. The repetitive "boogie-woogie" bass line, played with the left hand, was soon added, usually complemented by a stomping foot. If the player was blessed with a powerful voice, the package was complete. He could work alone, keep the house happy, and pocket the whole take himself.

Piano players could make the most money in the red-light districts of big cities: St. Louis, Memphis, New Orleans, Louisville, Cincinnati, and, of course, Chicago. In St. Louis, the sporting district along Market, Chestnut and Targee streets was one of the few places where black and white mixed, and a popular performer there could make a good living. Women worked as prostitutes, and men worked as musicians. To respectable people, there wasn't much difference between the two professions.

This was the music and life that attracted Roosevelt Sykes. An orphan, he spent school years with relatives in St. Louis and summers on his grandfather's farm outside

Roosevelt Sykes, producer Bob Koester and an unidentified drummer during a 1970 recording session.

Helena, Arkansas. He knew the rural life and he knew the alternative. As a young teenager, Sykes ran away from home to become a musician, playing piano in the barrelhouses around Helena and other Mississippi River towns as far south as Lake Providence, Louisiana.

Short and stocky, with a face like a bulldog, Sykes had a big voice and a heavy foot. He played all kinds of blues and other popular music, too, whatever his listeners wanted to hear. He could keep a crowd jumping until dawn at the country honky-tonks, but he always wanted more. He knew all about the big city, St. Louis. He had seen it as a

boy, and it was there that he headed as a young man, quickly finding his way to the roughest, most lawless parts of town.

Roosevelt Sykes was home at last and he knew it. This was the life for him! The city, especially its seamy side, was where he belonged, and life was good. His sweet way with the piano earned him a comfortable living, and his sweet way with the women earned him a nickname he wore proudly for the rest of his life: "Honeydripper." He even managed several of the honky-tonk saloons in which he performed.

After a few years in the St. Louis area, Sykes settled into a regular job at a little barrelhouse across the river in East St. Louis, Illinois. The gig paid him room, board, and a dollar a night. One afternoon in 1929, the twenty-three-year-old Sykes happened into a record store owned by Jesse Johnson, the St. Louis talent scout for a New York record company. Sykes played a few songs on Johnson's piano, and Johnson offered him a recording deal on the spot. They left for New York at eight o'clock the next morning. Sykes recorded four songs during that session, including "Forty-four Blues," one of his biggest hits.

He was paid fifteen hundred dollars for the session. "Fifteen hundred dollars and I been working for a dollar and a dollar and a half a night all my life," recalled Sykes in a 1980 interview. "And in just a few minutes, a guy give me fifteen hundred dollars. Money going to kill you, too much of it dropped on you at one time." It would kill some people maybe, but not Honeydripper. He used the money to buy a house in St. Louis and launch a bootlegging business there. (Prohibition was in effect until 1933.) Along with Big Joe Williams, Peetie Wheatstraw, and Charlie Jordan, he also kept a room at Seventeenth and O'Fallon for rehearsals and general hanging out.

As much as Sykes liked St. Louis, it couldn't hold him. He traveled to New York and Chicago frequently to make records, recording more than two hundred songs before World War II, almost all his own compositions. He also toured, appearing in the gambling dens and speakeasies of Memphis, Louisville, Cincinnati, and Chicago where, according to Sykes, "you could play the blues from Twenty-ninth Street up to Thirty-fifth" on the city's South Side.

In 1941, he moved his base of operations to Chicago, where he fronted a big band for several years. Always sensitive to audience tastes, Sykes believed big bands were the coming trend. During this period, he also played in a combo with Memphis Minnie Douglas and her husband at the time, Little Son Joe Lawlars. Sykes was even the house pianist for Decca Records during several of his Chicago years and accompanied many well-known blues artists such as Lonnie Johnson.

Through it all, Sykes was constantly writing and recording new songs. Many of his compositions commented on current events. In 1941, his "Training Camp Blues" encouraged young army recruits to "take your mind off your wife and put it on Uncle Sam." (Since he was thirty-five, Sykes was not eligible to fight.) In 1948, he made "Southern Blues," which urged blacks disillusioned by life in the North to return to their southern roots and old way of life. He sang, "Cotton prices going higher, and I ain't got no time to lose. Old Dixieland is jumping; I've got those southern blues."

His first recording and big hit, "Forty-four Blues," tells a somber tale about a man who catches his woman with another lover and dispatches them both with his gun, a .44-caliber revolver. "I wore my forty-four so long, Lord, it made my shoulder sore," he moans. By the end of the song, number "44" has appeared again as the number on his prison-cell door.

The Honeydripper's record sales started to dip in the early 1950s, and he moved his home from Chicago to New Orleans. There he influenced Fats Domino and other local artists. Sykes recorded infrequently during that decade, but soon discovered Europe's fascination with the blues. He toured and recorded there often, beginning in 1961; made records in England, Germany, and Denmark; did films in Belgium and France; and appeared on the stage everywhere. In the United States, he became a regular on the folk and blues festival circuit, working steadily right up until his death in 1983 from a heart attack. His piano technique influenced such later artists as Memphis Slim, Pinetop Perkins, Otis Spann, and many others.

Roosevelt Sykes is often identified as a transitional figure, connecting the rural and urban blues traditions. His greatest legacy, however, lies in the hundreds of recordings he made during his fifty-year career, all of which are available today on CD.

LITTLE BROTHER MONTGOMERY

Until his death in 1985, Little Brother Montgomery was a living link to the very beginnings of blues and jazz piano, one of the last pre-World War II greats. His constant, steady, and gentlemanly presence on the Chicago scene after 1940 influenced several generations of musicians. In particular, he was a lifelong inspiration to Willie Dixon, the primary architect of the successful Chicago electric blues sound of the early 1950s, and the primary exporter of that sound to the rest of the world.

Born in 1906, Eurreal Montgomery was called "Little Brother" by his family because he was always very small and had a

Performing, early 1960s.

youthful appearance. Willie Dixon saw him for the first time in about 1922 in Vicksburg, Mississippi, when Dixon was seven years old and Montgomery was sixteen, playing piano with a brass band on the back of wagon pulled by mules. Dixon was impressed by his music and also by his friendliness. Montgomery always shook hands with the little children and was so small himself that Dixon thought they were about the same age.

Little Brother Montgomery was born and raised in a pine-timber town north of New Orleans. Near the town's sawmill was a juke joint run by Montgomery's father. It wasn't fancy, but it had a piano, and every week another piano player would come through, including many of the best musicians from New Orleans. Little Eurreal studied at their elbows. By the age of five, he was playing piano, and by the age of eleven, he was working, making his way through all the lumber and turpentine camps, roadhouses, and honky-tonks of Louisiana and Mississippi, finally into New Orleans. He also traveled with an early jazz band out of Jackson, Mississippi, probably the group Dixon saw in Vicksburg.

According to Dixon's biography, Little Brother Montgomery was a regular at Curley's Barrelhouse in Vicksburg in 1922 or 1923. The barrelhouse was right next door to the restaurant owned by Dixon's mother. This was about the time Montgomery and two other pianists worked out a piano piece they called "Forty-Four Blues." They played it around the area to great success and taught it to some other piano players, including Roosevelt Sykes, who first recorded it and claimed it as his own. Montgomery later recorded it with a new name, "Vicksburg Blues," in what is usually considered the definitive treatment of the tune.

Stylistically, Montgomery was a "dudlow picker" or a "dudlow joe," a piano player with an up-tempo beat, faster than "barrel-house." The other musicians called this style "putting the dudlow to the blues." It later came to be called boogie-woogie and forms the backbone for much of jazz, blues, rhythm and blues, and rock and roll. Though the blues was his native style, Montgomery was always proud

Willie Dixon, the bassist, composer and producer who influenced a generation of Chicago blues artists, was himself strongly influenced by Little Brother Montgomery.

that he could play anything, in particular jazz and gospel.

By the end of the 1920s, Montgomery's travels took him to Chicago, where he played at rent parties and in small saloons. "Vicksburg Blues" was recorded first in 1930 at a session for Paramount, but the classic version is the one released by Bluebird in 1935, after Montgomery became part of the Lester Melrose group. Because of his versatility, Mont-

The dapper, lounge singer look, early 1960s.

gomery always found work in Chicago, both in the studios and the local nightspots, and he was just as likely to be playing jazz as blues.

As the Depression deepened in the early 1930s, Montgomery went back to Mississippi to form and lead his own dance band, which was successful until about 1939. Then it was back to Chicago for good. He put together a five-piece group—with trumpet, tenor sax, bass, and drums—and went to work at the Hollywood Show Lounge in the Loop for the next twelve years. After that, in the 1950s, he played on records with Otis Rush, Magic Sam Maghett, and other artists produced by Willie Dixon, and he was a major influence on Muddy Waters's pianist, Otis Spann.

Little Brother Montgomery inspired all of the Chicago blues pianists to hear and play other kinds of music than just the blues, which in turn influenced and gave variety to their music. Toward the end of his life, he spoke wistfully about the hundreds of piano players he had known in his youth, accomplished masters who had lived before recording technology was available so their artistry was now forgotten. In his music, Montgomery honored them by remembering the lessons they had taught him, and by sharing those gifts generously.

T-BONE WALKER

Money, or more usually the lack of it, has always influenced blues instrumentation. During slavery, when musical instruments of any kind were few and far between, and hands were usually occupied with cotton bolls, human voices were the main music-making tools. Next came stringed instruments like guitars and banjos, which were inexpensive or could be made from scavenged or inexpensive materials. Harmonicas also became popular because of their low cost and small size.

After slavery, when it became practical for a man to travel around and make a modest living playing music, one man singing his own songs and accompanying himself on an instrument was obviously the most efficient enter-tainment unit. Later, when playing louder was the way to perform solo in a bigger room where more money could be made, steel and then electric guitars were quickly adopted.

It was a change in economic conditions in the aftermath of World War II that set the stage for T-Bone Walker's emergence as a major blues star. The big bands that had ruled since the twenties had become too expensive to tour. In their place emerged scaled-down ensembles, consisting of a rhythm section (bass, drums, gui-tar, and/or piano, and/or organ) and a small horn section, backing a singer. The first of these new groups were formed on the West Coast among, and for, the GIs returning from the Pacific. If the ensemble had a singer who also played guitar and put on a lively and entertaining show, so much the better. That was Aaron Thibeaux "T-Bone" Walker.

In 1910, T-Bone Walker was born in Cass County, Texas. His mother, Movelia Jimerson, had lived her whole life in the state's rural northeastern corner, close to the Louisiana and Arkansas borders. Movelia's father was a laborer in a lumber mill. Her mother, a Cherokee Indian, raised fourteen children. Her hus-band, Rance Walker, was a sharecropper. Little T-Bone was her first and only child.

When T-Bone was about two years old ("T-Bone" was his mother's way of saying his middle name), Movelia left Cass County, and T-Bone's father, to put every-thing about the rural life behind her. She took her baby to Dallas, where they lived initially with Rance Walker's sister. Movelia and everyone else played guitars,

ATLANTIC
SD 8256

T-BONE
BLUES
BLUES
T-BONE
BLUES
T-BONE
T-BONE
T-BONE
T-BONE
BLUES

and professional musicians like Huddie Ledbetter and Blind Lemon Jefferson were regular houseguests when Walker was just a small child. Ledbetter, also known as Leadbelly, became famous as a folksinger and was one of the first African-Americans to play with white musicians before white audiences. Jefferson, then still a street performer, was to become one of the first country-blues recording stars. Walker remembered lying in bed as a child, deliberately staying awake for half the night, listening to their music.

When Movelia remarried, she naturally chose a musician, Marco Washington. When Walker was about ten, he and his stepfather played in a band consisting of the rest of the Washington brothers. The instrumentation included mandolins, guitars, and violins, all of which Walker could play. Everyone sang. Walker also danced.

This prepared him for his next job, a few months with a traveling medicine show. Walker was a natural performer, and other work followed, even though he was only a kid, his primary instrument still the banjo. As a teenager, he finally got a guitar so he could imitate his idol, Lonnie Johnson, who recorded with Louis Armstrong's band.

When Walker was about nineteen, he entered a talent contest at the Majestic Theater in Dallas. The prize was one week as a member of Cab Calloway's big band. He won, worked the week, and also landed a quick record deal with Columbia. The two sides he cut were old-time country-blues songs that showed the influence of Blind Lemon Jefferson. Unfortunately, Columbia never did very well with its country-blues series. The records went nowhere, and Columbia did not call him back.

All through this period, Walker belonged to a sixteen-piece dance band he had joined while still in high school. When he quit, a kid named Charlie Christian took his place. Years later, Christian became one of the most significant guitarists in jazz through his work with Benny Goodman.

In 1934, Walker met the woman to whom he would be married for the rest of his life, Vida Lee. Not long after their wedding, Walker moved to Los Angeles, where there was more local club work. By moving to California in search of a better life, Walker and thousands of other African-American Texans paralleled the Mississippi black migration to Chicago. The choice of destination was determined principally by where the trains went.

Vi Walker did not follow her husband to Los Angeles, even when he started to make money. She continued to live in Dallas, but they saw each other frequently, since he was always traveling. Two of Walker's lifelong personal problems, drinking and gambling, caused friction in the marriage but never split them up. Due to his drinking, Walker had constant trouble with stomach ulcers, beginning when he was a teenager. As for his gambling, "Blackjack," a Ray Charles song, is about the time Charles won two thousand dollars from Walker in an all-night poker game.

Twelve years into their marriage, the Walkers had their only child, a daughter named Bernita. Walker was by all accounts an enthusiastic parent and sometimes took Bernita along on tours. The other woman in Walker's life was his mother, who lived with him for most of his adult years.

Meanwhile, back in the mid-1930s, in addition to his new home and new wife, Walker had discovered something else brand-new: the electric guitar. The original idea was just to make the instrument louder, even though the first ones weren't much louder than a steel guitar, also invented for that purpose. Walker, however, understood instinctively the full potential of this new instrument and monitored its development closely. Walker, Charlie Christian, and several others would soon use it to revolutionize both blues and jazz guitar, introducing a style of single-note solos in which the guitarist plays runs similar to horn parts. This style, which for the blues matured in the hands of B. B. King, has become the dominant lead-guitar technique in jazz, blues, rock, country, and virtually every other subset of popular music.

Another unusual, though much less influential, characteristic of Walker's playing was the way he held his guitar perpendicular to his body rather than parallel. He also went through a period in the early 1940s when he did not play guitar onstage at all, but was the featured singer only, including a long stint in residence at Harlem's legendary Apollo Theater. This changed for good when he came to Chicago to mount a show at the Rhumboogie Club, a posh nightspot patterned after Harlem's Cotton Club and co-owned by Joe Louis, the boxer. In what today might be called a Las Vegas-style revue, Walker sang, danced, and played electric guitar in front of a big band.

Also in the 1940s, Walker started to record again. The most productive period of his career was the decade just after the war's end. Most of his sessions were held in Los Angeles and were some of the first for that city's fledgling music industry. In 1947, he wrote and recorded the song that would become his trademark tune and biggest hit, "Stormy Monday."

It was also during this period that he fronted one of the first "small big bands," which were basically a rhythm section with horns. Walker led one of the first postwar, West Coast, "jump blues" bands that also called their music rhythm and blues. These groups, many headed by transplanted Texans like T-Bone Walker, played a smooth, sophisticated, blues-based dance music that influenced the development of jazz and led to the creation of rock and roll. For a time, T-Bone Walker was their king.

By the late 1950s, stomach ulcers, aggravated by Walker's excessive drinking, put him into the hospital more and more often, leading to frequent cancellations. He finally fired his band and checked into the hospital to have the operation he had postponed for years. When he finally was able to work again, he appeared with the Count Basie Band, then joined a group of bluesmen that included John Lee Hooker, Muddy Waters, Memphis Slim, Willie Dixon, Sonny Terry, Brownie McGhee, and several others for the first American Folk Blues Festival tour of Europe.

Walker spent much of the 1960s performing in Europe and also recorded there, but he continued to have many fans in the United States, too, even though they saw him much less frequently. In 1970, he received a Grammy Award for his album, "Good Feeling." He worked on and off thereafter, as much as his declining health permitted. In 1975, he died following a stroke. He was sixty-four.

Walker was an important influence on untold numbers of later artists in blues and most other popular music forms for his guitar playing, his vocal style, and his stage act. Buddy Guy and B. B. King both credit him as a major influence on their guitar technique, and while King's vocals more closely resemble Walker's, Guy has adopted many of his outrageous stage stunts. Chuck Berry also copied much of T-Bone Walker's act, especially his guitar-played-behind-the-head, splits-to-the-floor, hop-back-up routine. Considered a father of both the Austin-based Texas blues and the LA-based West Coast blues, Walker influenced guitarists such as Albert King, Freddie King, Stevie Ray Vaughn, Albert Collins, Eric Clapton, Jeff Beck, Jimmy Page, and Otis Rush. Little Walter Jacobs credits Walker for shaping his vocal style.

Although some of his orchestral arrangements sound terribly corny today, Walker's guitar solos are always impeccable and frequently breathtaking. His lead runs are a complete graduate course in contemporary guitar technique. His music sounds familiar, even if you have never heard it before, because everyone has copied from him.

HOWLIN' WOLF

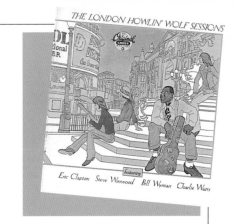

THE LONDON HOWLIN' WOLF SESSIONS

featuring Eric Clapton Steve Winwood Bill Wyman Charlie Watts

C hester Arthur Burnett never cared much for his famous nickname. Once, in the 1960s, he complained bitterly to a *Downbeat* writer about a profile of him which emphasized the obvious parallels between the man and the beast: his restless prowling onstage, the ferocity of his guitar playing, his often-bared incisors, and, of course, his howling vocal style. "You made me sound like an animal," Wolf protested, but what could he really say? Everyone who knew him, or ever saw him perform, agreed that the nickname fit perfectly, especially with his deep, raspy, powerful voice.

After Howlin' Wolf came to Chicago in the 1950s, some friends and fellow musicians from the old days down south continued to call him "Foots," an earlier nickname referring to his size-sixteen shoes, but to everyone else he was simply "Wolf." Certainly it was better than his given name, a tribute to the twenty-first president.

Like so many facts about the early life of this extremely influential bluesman, the origins of his nickname are somewhat obscure. Wolf himself supplied a couple of different explanations over the years—about a grandfather's scary wolf tales, about his own "wolfish" mischief as a child—but the apparent truth is more prosaic. Justifiably unhappy with "Big Foot Chester" as a performing handle, Burnett appropriated the nickname of an older bluesman, John T. Smith, who had adopted the name "The Howling Wolf" after his 1930 record of that song became popular. By the time Chester Burnett came along, Smith had faded into obscurity so no one objected when Big Foot Chester rechristened himself Howlin' Wolf.

The backgrounds of some legendary bluesmen are unknown because they died before anyone cared about such things, but Wolf was the focus of intense interest, especially during the last twenty years of his life. Questions about his past were asked often, but they were seldom answered, or the answers given were vague and contradictory. His brother-in-law and musical mentor, the second Sonny Boy Williamson (real name: Alex "Rice" Miller), was similarly vague about his roots and, like Wolf, also appropriated the name of an older, more famous performer. (The first "Sonny Boy" was murdered in Chicago in 1948.)

This amazing series of photographs was taken during a mid-1960s Howlin' Wolf performance at the legendary Silvio's Lounge on Chicago's West Side. Silvio's was a long-time blues staple and for many years was Howlin' Wolf's Chicago headquarters.

Blues researchers are pretty sure that Chester Arthur Burnett was born in 1910, possibly in Clay County, Mississippi. When he was about thirteen, the family moved west into the Delta and onto the Young and Morrow Plantation near Ruleville, Mississippi. At eighteen, Wolf was given his first guitar by his father, and his first guitar lessons by the seminal blues master, Charlie Patton. In addition to Patton's guitar style, Wolf also began to imitate the older man's stage antics. To whip his audience into a frenzy, Patton would beat his guitar like a drum, pick it behind his back or with his teeth, or roll around on the stage while he sang.

Wolf's other main teacher was Miller. When he started dating Wolf's half-sister, Mary, Wolf pestered him for harmonica lessons, which Miller gave as quickly as possible so he could get back to romance. At that time, Wolf also heard the music of other local performers like Son House and the Mississippi Sheiks, as well as records by Blind Lemon Jefferson.

A slow but persistent student, Wolf was soon good enough to take occasional breaks from his farming to play professionally on the regional juke-joint, country-supper, fish-fry circuit. When his father moved the family across the river to Arkansas, Wolf went along but continued to play whenever he could, often with Miller (who by now was calling himself Sonny Boy Williamson) and the legendary Robert Johnson. As the 1930s ended, Williamson got a radio job in Helena, Arkansas, Johnson got murdered by a jealous husband, and Wolf got drafted.

His four years in the Army during World War II were another period of his life Wolf would never discuss, except to say that he spent most of the time stationed in Seattle, Washington. After the war, he farmed with his father for a while, then on his own. He was married to his second wife (the first had died) and thirty-eight years old when he finally decided to try music full-time in 1948.

The venue he chose was West Memphis, Arkansas, a rough-and-tumble, wide-open town of gambling dens, brothels and bars. The bands Wolf assembled were all made up of musicians twenty years younger, but he selected them well. They included at various times Matt "Guitar"

Murphy, Junior Parker, and James Cotton, all of whom went on to enjoy major blues careers of their own. Every night Wolf played the West Memphis joints, and every afternoon he performed on KWEM, the local radio station, either with his young band or spinning records as a disc jockey. He even sold advertising for the station.

Howlin' Wolf was finally a star, albeit a regional one, but he had still not recorded. That changed in 1951 when he was "discovered" by the much-younger Ike Turner, who had just had a number-one rhythm-and-blues hit with "Rocket 88," often described as the first rock-and-roll song. Turner arranged for Wolf to record with Sam Phillips in Memphis (the same producer who launched Elvis Presley and Jerry Lee Lewis), and the result was a hit. Soon Wolf was on his way to the blues capital of the

world, Chicago, with an exclusive contract to record for the Chess brothers.

When Wolf arrived in Chicago, he was forty-two years old. The first couple of years were difficult as neither hit records nor lucrative club dates seemed to come his way. By 1954, conditions had improved enough for him to return south and fetch some of his old band members, including guitarist Hubert Sumlin, with whom he collaborated profitably for the rest of his career. Wolf treated Sumlin like a son and between them, they were able to create a musical formula that finally made Howlin' Wolf a superstar.

Wolf's other key collaborator in Chicago was Willie Dixon, the producer, bass player, and house composer at Chess Records. Dixon was one of very few men who could successfully tell Wolf what to do. Howlin'

Wolf was a huge man—six feet, three-inches tall and about 275 pounds—but Dixon was even bigger: just as tall, 300-plus pounds, and a former professional boxer. Sometimes their disagreements got heated, resulting in pushing and shoving, and Dixon putting Wolf "in the collar," as he called it, but they never actually came to blows.

By the 1960s, with Dixon's songs and Sumlin's music, Howlin' Wolf had finally become one of a handful of blues superstars. In general, though, the popularity of blues was starting to fade as increasingly affluent and urbanized black audiences turned to more sophisticated music like soul and jazz. At the same time, American teenagers, both black and white, only wanted rock and roll. Wolf, Muddy Waters, Little Walter, J.B. Lenoir, and Wolf's old running buddy, Sonny Boy Williamson, were the only blues singers left on the Chess roster by the end of the decade, as the company shifted its emphasis to much more profitable rock-and-roll acts like Chuck Berry and Bo Diddley.

As usual, it was Willie Dixon who found the solution. Through contacts he had made with several promoters, Dixon was able to book lucrative European tours for himself, Waters, Wolf, Williamson, Otis Spann, Buddy Guy, and many others. In 1964, Dixon booked the first blues tour ever to go behind the Iron Curtain, taking Wolf, Sumlin, and Sunnyland Slim along with him. They played East Germany, Czechoslovakia, Poland, and a part of rural Poland that they thought was Russia.

Payment for the tour was to be half in U.S. funds and half in the local currency, which was not convertible. All the musicians were instructed to spend the local money there, but Wolf couldn't find anything he wanted to buy and insisted that his share be donated to the local YMCA. The German promoter who had arranged the trip was unable to convince Wolf that the Young Men's Christian Association did not have any branches in communist countries.

When he was back in Chicago, Wolf's performing home was Silvio's on Lake Avenue on the West Side. This was another aspect of his long-running rivalry with Muddy Waters, who ruled the South Side blues clubs like Pepper's and the Checkerboard Lounge. Willie Dixon wrote for both men, and each complained that the composer gave his best songs to the other. Dixon took to applying reverse psychology, claiming to Wolf that the songs he offered him had actually been written for Waters and vice versa.

In the early to mid-1960s, the team of Wolf, Sumlin, and Dixon had a string of hits, including "Spoonful," "Back Door Man," "The Red Rooster," and "I Ain't Superstitious." "Back Door Man" was their biggest success and became Wolf's signature tune. These were also the records that, along with the European tours, brought Wolf and Dixon to the attention of English blues rockers like the Rolling Stones, the Animals, Fleetwood Mac, and Led Zeppelin, and through them to American bands like the Doors.

By the late 1960s, the blues could be heard in Chicago's white neighborhoods. One club, Big John's, featured Buddy Guy and Junior Wells every Monday night, Muddy Waters on Wednesday, and Howlin' Wolf on Thursday. A young, white blues band led by Paul Butterfield and Elvin Bishop played there on the weekends. While Wolf was entertaining the white audiences at Big John's, another aspiring young, white bluesman, Steve Miller, was trying to take over Wolf's gigs at Club Melody or the Blue Flame.

As the 1970s began, Howlin' Wolf turned sixty. He recorded an interesting album in London with Eric Clapton, Ringo Starr, Ian Stewart, Charlie Watts, Steve Winwood, Bill Wyman, and, of course, Hubert Sumlin, reprising many of his biggest hits. It was released in 1971 as "The London Howlin' Wolf Sessions." At about the same time, Wolf suffered the first of several heart attacks. In 1973, he was seriously injured in an automobile accident, from which he never fully recovered. Chester "Howlin' Wolf" Burnett died during surgery on January 10, 1976, in an Illinois Veteran's Administration hospital.

A mediocre instrumentalist and an expressive, but limited, singer, Howlin' Wolf's success was due more to his personality and sheer will than his musical skills. One critic's apt description of Wolf's performing style was "feral intensity." He was probably the single most successful interpreter of Willie Dixon's songs, which embodied the Chicago electric-blues style. Most of all, it was Wolf, along with archrival Muddy Waters, who was most responsible for broadening the blues audience across racial and national lines. Today it is practically impossible to discuss the blues without mentioning Howlin' Wolf. That at least Wolf would have liked.

ROBERT JOHNSON

For an artist, death at a young age is often a long-term career advantage, especially when the individual's early output is outstanding. Death eliminates the pesky creative troughs and bad decisions that can haunt a longer career. James Dean and Marilyn Monroe never appeared on *Love Boat* and Buddy Holly never had to resort to a "rock revival" tour. Images of them are frozen in time, at or near their prime. Imagine, for example, how different Judy Garland's legacy might be if she had died after *Easter Parade* in 1948, instead of twenty years later.

But when there is so little paint on the canvas, the temptation for many to fill it in with their own hopes, fears, and needs is practically irresistible. Robert Johnson has carried that freight more than any other bluesman. He is probably the most researched and speculated-about singer in blues history. His family, ex-lovers and fellow musicians have all been interviewed at length, beginning shortly after his death in 1938. Beyond that research, his entire legacy is forty-one takes of twenty-nine songs, recorded in 1936 and 1937.

Had Robert Johnson lived into the postwar era, who knows what direction his musical career might have taken? He was just twenty-six years old when he was murdered in 1938. Had he lived, he would have been thirty-five in 1946, about the same age as Lightnin' Hopkins and T-Bone Walker, and just a little older than Muddy Waters and John Lee Hooker. To some commentators, Waters only ascended to his throne as father of the electrified Chicago blues because Johnson was not available for the job.

The wishful speculation of many critics is that if he had lived longer, Johnson would have jump-started rock and roll. One of his supposed prerock innovations was the transposition

of the boogie-woogie or "walking" bass line, typical of blues piano, to the guitar. The blues recordings of the 1940s that are usually named as the first examples of rock and roll also possess this characteristic. Listen to Lightnin' Hopkins on "Play with Your Poodle" from 1947 and Johnson on "Thirty-Two—Twenty Blues" from 1936. Although there is no evidence that Hopkins, Chuck Berry, or any other early rockers were inspired directly by Johnson, few other blues guitarists played the way he did in the 1930s.

Does that make him the father

Robert Junior Lockwood, a superb guitarist, spent much of his career in the posthumous shadow of his coincidental namesake, Robert Johnson. Only four years older than Lockwood, Johnson lived with Lockwood's mother for several years and was the younger man's first important teacher in blues guitar technique.

of rock and roll? Aside from his legend, Johnson is important primarily because his music had a major impact on Eric Clapton, Keith Richards, and other English blues rockers of the 1960s. The blues revival of the 1950s had prompted Columbia Records, which had obtained the Johnson masters from the American Record Company, to release an album of sixteen Johnson songs in 1961, entitled "King of the Delta Blues Singers." A more complete collection, on two long-play records, was released in 1966 and 1970. Rolling Stones founder Brian Jones had the 1961 compilation and played it for Keith Richards, who was blown away. When the 1966 set reached England, it contained "Love In Vain," which the Stones recorded a few years later on their "Let It Bleed" album, in a country-tinged arrangement inspired by Byrds guitarist Gram Parsons.

Clapton, then a member of Cream, also recorded a modified Johnson tune, "Crossroads," on 1968's "Wheels of Fire." To him, listening to Johnson for the first time was "almost like a religious experience," and Clapton is one of those who consider Johnson to be "the most important blues musician who ever lived." Clapton's hugely successful 1992 "Unplugged" album contains two Johnson songs, "Walkin' Blues" and "Malted Milk."

Robert Johnson was born in 1911. Nothing is known about his father, Noah Johnson, except his name, probably because Julia Dodds, Robert's mother, was married to someone else at the time. Her husband, Charlie Dodds, Jr., was unusual among Mississippi African-Americans because he owned the land he farmed in Hazlehurst, Mississippi, where Robert was born. In 1907, Charlie Dodds got on the wrong side of a prominent local white family and was forced to flee to Memphis, where he changed his name to Spencer. He took his mistress and some of his children by both women along, but Julia stayed behind.

She left Hazlehurst shortly after Robert's birth. When Johnson was a baby, they lived for a time in migrant labor camps; then Johnson lived in Memphis with the Doddses, both with and without his mother. When he was about seven, Johnson rejoined his mother and her new husband in Robinsonville, Mississippi, in Tunica County, where he lived into adulthood.

Robinsonville is hard by the Mississippi River, about halfway between Memphis and Helena, Arkansas. Clarksdale is a little further south in Coahoma County. When Johnson was growing up, this relatively small area was home to many of the men who became blues legends: Charlie Patton, Son House, Willie Brown,

Sonny Boy Williamson (Rice Miller), and many others. Howlin' Wolf was still Chester Burnett in those days and just a year older than Johnson. Coming up a handful of years later were John Lee Hooker and Muddy Waters.

House was the first local musician who really impressed the teenage Robert Johnson, but Lonnie Johnson's records were another important influence. Although Robert and Lonnie were not related, Robert began to use his father's surname (he had been using either Dodds or Spencer) at about the same time he discovered Lonnie Johnson's music, and he wasn't above suggesting they were kin. When he started going by his first two initials, R.L., he told everyone the "L" stood for Lonnie, even though Leroy was really his middle name.

Robert Johnson tried to learn guitar at the feet of Son House and Willie Brown but was largely unsuccessful. In 1929, he married Virginia Travis, who died in childbirth a year later. Distraught over her death, Johnson returned to Hazlehurst, in the southern part of the state, to search for his father. There he met a bluesman named Ike Zinnerman, who became his most important teacher. When he returned to Robinsonville about eighteen months later, he could play anything, leading House and the others to conclude that he had sold his soul to the devil. Johnson encouraged this myth, a fairly common claim among bluesmen, and wrote a song about it, "Cross Road Blues."

Even among his itinerant musician colleagues, Robert Johnson was known as a traveler. Although he made Helena his base, he never stayed anyplace for very long and toured the region continuously, either solo or with fellow bluesmen like Sonny Boy Williamson and Howlin' Wolf. One hastily arranged trip with two other guitarists, Johnny Shines and Calvin Frazier (who was wanted for murder), took him to St. Louis, Chicago, and Detroit, where they crossed the bridge and also played in Windsor, Ontario. Frazier stayed in Detroit, but Johnson and Shines went on to New York and New Jersey before returning to the Delta.

Although this tour was not formally arranged, Johnson found playing jobs along the way on the strength of his record, "Terraplane Blues," which had been recorded in San Antonio, Texas, in 1936. With four thousand copies sold, it was a minor hit and made Johnson a rising star, always able to find work. It also led to a second recording date, in Dallas, in 1937. All of the recordings we have of him come from those two sessions. Johnson recorded solo on both occasions, but was rumored to have played in groups, too. When discovered in the 1960s, this fact fueled more speculation about his prerock experimentation, even though combos were not particularly rare at the time.

While on the road, Johnson was always seeking female companionship. This has been a staple in the lives of traveling musicians probably since the beginning of time. Robert Johnson, unfortunately, was both more successful and more reckless at attracting women than most. His final dalliance, with the wife of a juke-joint owner, earned him a bottle of strychnine-poisoned whiskey. Though he survived the poison, Johnson contracted pneumonia and died a few days later, on August 16, 1938.

Johnson's legend may have become a bit oversized in the fifty-plus years since his death, but his music is still important. We are fortunate that he was recorded by people who simply turned on the machines and let him play. Listening to those tracks today gives us a richly detailed snapshot not only of Johnson's music at that moment but also of the Delta blues milieu as it sounded in 1936–37, just a decade before its discovery by the wider world following World War II. Johnson lives forever in that moment.

Furry Lewis demonstrates the Delta bottleneck guitar technique practiced by Robert Johnson and many other Mississippi bluesmen.

LIGHTNIN' HOPKINS

One of the frustrations of studying the blues is the nagging suspicion that we may have missed it all. Perhaps everything we have heard is just a remnant, an echo, already past its prime and corrupted by mainstream culture before it got to us. We know almost nothing about the way the music sounded before the mid-1920s, and the blues artists we're aware of from then until the end of World War II are the very small number who were "discovered" by white record producers and folklore researchers, not necessarily a representative sample.

Lightnin' Hopkins performing at the University of Chicago in 1965.

As for the commercial blues recordings made before World War II, most were heavily produced by white record-company executives, so aesthetic and marketing judgments made by whites shaped much of what is on them. Were these artists and their songs the best available? The most original? The most authentic? Are they representative? We have no way of knowing what music really ruled the juke-joint and picnic circuit until after World War II.

After the war, a proliferation of small companies, some run by blacks, began to record the blues, and whites in large numbers also became interested. Among these new white fans, a quest for "authenticity" began. Hard-core blues fans sought out the oldest living musicians and asked them to sing the oldest songs they could remember. This quest for authenticity made the musical pedigree of a bluesman important to a fan who craved a hint of pure blues as it had existed before white culture discovered it. Thus the credibility of Sam "Lightnin'" Hopkins was buoyed by his early associations with Blind Lemon Jefferson and Texas Alexander, in the same way that Muddy Waters was linked to Son House, and Howlin' Wolf to Charlie Patton. It is the reason Big Bill Broonzy was billed as "the last blues singer alive" when he toured Europe in the 1950s. Broonzy died in

1958, and the next year, in his seminal history, *The Country Blues,* Samuel Charters passed the torch to Hopkins, declaring him "perhaps the last of the great blues singers."

Among black audiences in the 1950s, a similar concern manifested itself in the debate between defenders of old-time "country" blues and young fans of the new "urban" sound, typified by Muddy Waters. To many, Lightnin' Hopkins represented the more authentic, down-home, "gut bucket" country blues older fans preferred. This is a little hard to understand now, since Hopkins played electric guitar, too, and could rock the blues as hard as Waters. Hopkins probably explained the real difference when he complained that Chicago men only sang about women. He sang about women and whiskey and hard luck and many other things: farming, weather, bad bosses, racial injustice, prison life, death, and war.

This conflict between fans of country and city blues was symbolized in the 1950s by an annual promotion run on WDIA, the influential, all-black radio station broadcasting from Memphis. For several years, "Mr. Blues," host of the station's popular "Wheelin' on Beale" show, ran an election for president of a fictional organization he called the Royal Amalgamated Association of Chitterling Eaters of America, Inc.,

for the Preservation of Good Country Blues. In the 1954 campaign, the candidates for president were Lightnin' Hopkins and Muddy Waters, and Mr. Blues was hardly neutral.

He appointed himself as Hopkins's campaign manager and, naturally, Hopkins won by a wide margin. It was all in fun because Waters was also popular on the station, but his music was too "city" for many older WDIA listeners. For their taste, Lightnin' Hopkins was just right.

The vast cotton country of East Texas is a long way from the Mississippi Delta, but conditions for black laborers there were similar, and a blues culture developed. Sam Hopkins was born in 1912 in tiny Centerville, Texas, a cotton-farming community between Dallas and Houston, about 120 miles from each. Sam was the third of six children, all musical, and his older brothers, John Henry (eleven years older) and Joel (eight years older), were his first musical influences. They had been taught by their father, Abe, who died in a violent card game when Sam was only three.

At about the age of eight, Hopkins had his first encounter with the legendary Blind Lemon Jefferson, who was then about twenty-three. Jefferson was performing at the Sunday afternoon picnic sponsored by the General Association of Baptist Churches at Buffalo, Texas, about seventeen

miles from the Hopkins farm.
Although the string of records
that would make him immortal
were still more than six years in
the future, Jefferson already had
a big reputation in the area.
When the Hopkins family arrived
at the picnic, the little boy with the
guitar quickly found the young
blind man and fell in to playing
behind him. Jefferson barked,

"Boy, you got to play it right," but softened his tone when he realized Hopkins's age. Later, as a teenager, Hopkins accompanied Jefferson and served as his eyes when they traveled the region performing together. (Jefferson froze to death in Chicago in the winter of 1929–30 at the age of thirty-two.)

The other Hopkins connection to a legend of the earlier era was his association with a much older cousin, Alger "Texas" Alexander, a singer whom he accompanied on and off from 1926 until Alexander's death in 1954. In Alexander's vocals, you can hear the hoots and hollers of field hands and prison work gangs,

the music that led to the blues. Alexander made sixty-seven recordings between 1927 and 1934, accompanied by Lonnie Johnson on the first twenty of them. It was the legacy of this association with Jefferson and Alexander, as much as his own artistry, that got Sam "Lightnin'" Hopkins onto the blues-revival bandwagon beginning in the late 1950s.

Through the 1920s, '30s, and most of the '40s, Sam Hopkins was a farmer who played music on weekends. He also liked to drink, gamble, fight, and chase women. He got into a few scrapes and had scars on his ankles from prison leg irons to prove he had lived the life. During those years, most of his songs were sung to the back of a mule. One day in 1946, when he was thirty-four years old, Hopkins tied the mule to a tree and walked away. It was the same year B. B. King abandoned his mule and headed to Memphis.

World War II had just ended when Hopkins made his way to Houston, the city in Texas with the largest black population. Like Memphis in the Delta, most of the region's cotton was shipped through Houston, so blacks could find jobs there on the docks and in the railroad yards, sawmills, textile plants, and stockyards. The money wasn't great, but a man could make a living and still have

Lightnin' Hopkins performing at the University of Chicago in 1965.

a big time on Saturday night.

As was true in most U.S. cities at the time, the place where African-American musicians found work was in the city's vice district, a part of the Fourth Ward. Here there were dozens of small honky-tonks and taverns where a bluesman could make some money, or at least earn a meal and some drinks. Although Lightnin' Hopkins was to enjoy significant fame and success over the next thirty-six years, he continued to live and perform in the poor, working-class neighborhoods of Houston for the rest of his life. His nickname came from an early recording partnership with a piano player named Wilson "Thunder" Smith. Their manager thought "Thunder and Lightning" would look good on a marquee, but the name also fit Hopkins's rapid-fire playing style. The final "g" was eventually and universally dropped.

Hopkins recorded in bursts of incredible productivity. He was so prolific when he was in the mood to record that he consistently failed to honor his exclusive contracts, which led to a constant turnover of recording companies. Since he preferred straight cash buyouts to any kind of royalty arrangements, there was no way for the companies to enforce the contracts or encourage his loyalty.

From the beginning of his recording career, Hopkins showed an amazing range. He performed on acoustic and electric guitar, alone or with a small combo, and sometimes on solo dates, he wore taps on his shoes and added percussion that way. On a few recordings, he accompanied himself on piano or organ instead of guitar. He also had a vast repertoire of material, most of it original, some of it composed on the spot from standard blues motifs.

He recorded many down-home country blues but also played urban blues, and some of his songs seem to anticipate rock and roll. "Play with Your Poodle," from a 1947 session with Hopkins on guitar, Thunder Smith on piano, and an unknown drummer, has been called one of the first rock-and-roll songs.

The first Lightnin' Hopkins records were local hits, but in 1950 his "Shotgun Blues" made it to number five on the national *Billboard* rhythm-and-blues chart. In 1952, he had his biggest national success with two songs at the same time, "Give Me Central 209" and "Coffee Blues," both of which peaked at number six.

Hopkins recorded as often as he could from 1946 until the mid-1950s, then took a few years off. When he returned in 1959, it was at the behest of a mostly white folk-music audience. He recorded constantly for about four years, took a few years off, and resumed recording in the mid- to late-1960s. He also performed regularly at festivals and universities and could have done more, especially internationally, but he hated to travel. As he approached his sixtieth birthday, with his fame and a modest fortune secure, Hopkins was content to live and play mostly in the Houston area.

In 1972, Hopkins collaborated with Taj Mahal on music for the film *Sounder,* and he performed at New York's Carnegie Hall. Thereafter, he worked less and less, playing a few festivals and universities, and he made one last tour of Europe in 1977. He slowed down because of his health and because he didn't really need the money anymore. He died in 1982 of cancer, six weeks before his seventieth birthday.

Lightnin' Hopkins influenced a diverse group of artists, from John Lee Hooker and Buddy Guy to Bob Dylan and Joan Baez. In the end, though, all of the famous associations throughout his career don't tell us very much. Was Hopkins just a very good student who had amazing teachers, making him merely a last vestigial link to the giants of a storied past? Or was he an astonishingly creative and skillful artist who took a little from his predecessors but mostly made his art from the world around him? Or was he both? We don't know the answer. All we have is his amazing music.

MUDDY WATERS

A complete lesson in the blues can be had in three minutes or less by listening to the Muddy Waters recording of "Long Distance Call" with Waters on guitar and vocals, Big Crawford on bass, and Little Walter on harmonica. In this one song, cut in Chicago in 1951, the whole history of the blues is heard, including its future. What becomes apparent is the reason that Muddy Waters is considered so important, both musically and symbolically.

The subject of "Long Distance Call" is frustrated love, the most common theme in blues lyrics. Some say it's the only theme in blues lyrics. Specifically, it is about the frustration of a man separated

At Pepper's Lounge in the early 1960s.

from his lover, a timeless lament but also a very real problem throughout the Delta Diaspora as thousands of blacks left loved ones in the South to seek opportunity in other regions. At the end of the song, the singer finally answers his ringing telephone but instead of hearing his lover's voice "to ease my worried mind" an unidentified "party" on the other end confirms the singer's worst fears, that "another mule is kicking in your stall."

The lyric style of "Long Distance Call" is very traditional. "Long Distance Moan," virtually the same song, was recorded in 1929 by Blind Lemon Jefferson. It uses the traditional AAB blues structure, a three-line verse in which the first line is repeated and then answered by the third. Waters usually avoided this pattern for his songs, in favor of the ABAB struc-

Cotton and Waters in an all-star show at the Chicago Civic Opera, mid-1960s.

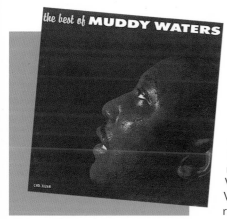

ture more typical of mainstream popular songs. Consequently, this was old-time music even for him. On the 1951 recording, Waters's vocal is pure, deep country blues—raw, plaintive, and heart-wrenching.

If the song had been recorded with Waters alone, accompanied by his acoustic guitar, it might have been indistinguishable from the Library of Congress field recordings he made ten years earlier on Stovall's Plantation in Mississippi. Instead, the first notes we hear are from Waters's *electric* guitar as Little Walter's in-your-face harmonica roars throughout, trading licks

with the voice and guitar interchangeably. The group sound is as tight as it can be, and it is easy to imagine someone like Led Zeppelin covering the song in a rock version.

That is the legacy of Muddy Waters. He personified, in his life and music, a common African-American heritage and experience, but he also anticipated the future. As such, he was the key link between the two. By 1951, he was already a model and leader among Chicago blues musicians and popular with African-American record buyers throughout the USA; but his creativity, passion, and authenticity, as well as his personal generosity and integrity, would eventually touch and inspire a most unlikely audience: white, working-class English teenagers like Mick Jagger, Keith Richards, and John Lennon

In 1915, Ollie Morganfield and Bertha Jones had a baby boy. They named him McKinley but his grandmother Ola, with whom he lived almost from birth, soon nicknamed him "Muddy." As an adult, McKinley Morganfield would travel far from his birthplace in Sharkey County, Mississippi, but his first journey at age three was probably the most significant. When Bertha died in 1918, Ola Jones moved her young grandson back to her home 100 miles to the north in Coahoma County. There, on the Stovall plantation near Clarksdale, Muddy's playmates completed his nickname, and he first heard the blues of Son House, one of the many now-famous bluesmen who lived and/or worked in the area

and who taught Muddy Waters how to play the blues.

Waters started with the harmonica as a child, but at about age seventeen he scraped together all the nickels and dimes he could to buy a used guitar for $2.50. The first time he played it, he made fifty cents and never looked back. "I always thought of myself as a musician," he recalled to an interviewer in 1964. "The different jobs I had back in Clarksdale and so forth, they were just temporary things. If I wasn't a good musician then, I felt that sooner or later I would be a good musician. I felt it in me."

In 1940, Waters thought he might be ready. He made a trip to St. Louis but soon returned to take care of his grandmother. In 1941, Alan Lomax arrived at Stovall's with sound recording equipment as part of a many-year project to document American folk music for the Library of Congress. Lomax knew about Son House, who was then almost forty and about Robert Johnson, who though he was just four years older than Waters, was already three years dead by 1941. Lomax did not know about the twenty-six-year-old Waters, but recorded him on the recommendation of local contacts. Waters showed up for the first recording session without a guitar, having lent his to a friend, but warmed quickly to

the sound and feel of Lomax's Martin.

Alan Lomax was so impressed with Muddy Waters that he recorded three songs, then returned the next summer to cut several more, both solo and with a small combo. "I was bowled over by his artistry," Lomax recalled in his 1993 memoirs. "He sang and played with such finesse, with such a mercurial and sensitive bond between voice and guitar, and he expressed so much tenderness in the way he handled his lyrics, that he went right beyond all his predecessors— Blind Lemon, Charley Patton, Robert Johnson, Son House, and Willie Brown."

In 1943, the Library of Congress released two of the songs Waters recorded, and Lomax sent him a copy of the seventy-eight rpm disc. Hearing himself for the first time was a revelation, and it prompted Waters to give the big city another try. After obtaining his grandmother's blessing, Muddy Waters caught the Illinois Central bound for Chicago. When he returned to Clarksdale a few years later, it was in triumph.

At first, Chicago did not embrace Muddy Waters or his style of music. Bebop jazz was all the rage, but Waters soon found the tiny neighborhood clubs where blues were still played. Big Bill Broonzy showed him around, and soon Waters joined the Sonny Boy Williamson band. He also picked

Muddy Waters and his harp player of the mid-1960s, James Cotton.

up a job driving a truck for a Venetian blind company.

By the time Waters arrived in Chicago, Broonzy, Lonnie Johnson, and Tampa Red were the top guitarists in town, and they were already playing electrics. Waters got one in 1944, a gift from an uncle. The decision to go electric was more practical than anything else; it was the only way to be heard.

Waters's first Chicago recording was made in 1945 or 1946, but released under the name James "Sweet Lucy" Carter. In 1946, Waters was also recorded by the legendary Lester Melrose, but those tracks were not released until almost thirty years later.

In 1947, he cut several sides for Leonard Chess, but those, too, sat on the shelf. In 1948, Chess recorded him again. This time he released the record, "I Can't Be Satisfied," and it was an instant smash, selling out 3,000 copies in about twenty-four hours. Muddy Waters was a star.

Now, instead of playing rent parties, Muddy Waters and his band were headlining the very best rooms in town—the Du Drop Lounge and the Boogie Woogie Inn. Waters assembled an all-star band and kept it together for many years. One key component was an eighteen-year-old street musician named Marion Walter Jacobs, aka "Little Walter," who would later front his own successful group. The drummer was Baby Face Leroy Foster, and Jimmy Rogers was on the other guitar.

During the early 1950s, the Muddy Waters Band played virtually every night at one of the clubs on Chicago's South Side, or they toured throughout the East and South. In 1953, Waters recorded the Willie Dixon song "Hoochie Coochie Man," and it became his trademark tune. The record sold 4,000 copies in the first week and spent several weeks on the national Rhythm and Blues Top 10 Chart. It was his biggest hit.

In the mid-1950s, everything started to change. A new kind of music, rock and roll, was attracting teenagers of both races. Sales of blues records started to fall. Meanwhile, in England, teenagers like Mick Jagger, Keith Richards, and John Lennon (ages fifteen, fifteen, and eighteen respectively in 1958) were hearing Muddy Waters and other electric blues artists on rare, imported records and forming bands dedicated to playing blues music. A European tour in 1958 broadened his overseas audience and also introduced him to jazz audiences on both continents. In 1959, he played Carnegie Hall with James Cotton (harmonica) and Memphis Slim (piano).

When the new decade began, Muddy Waters was forty-five years old. He was an established, though fading, star in the African-American community but was still being discovered by ever-larger white audiences. Some of his new fans were students from the University of Chicago, which was not far from the South Side Clubs. These included the founders of 1960s rock-blues bands such as Paul Butterfield, Mike Bloomfield, and Steve Miller.

The 1960s were a strange time for Muddy Waters. He was hailed as a "living legend" at music festivals and by groups like the Rolling Stones, the Beatles, Jimi Hendrix, Steve Miller, and many others. He even hosted a show on a Chicago radio station. Meanwhile, his record company tried to "update" his sound, once with organ and horns and soul-style arrangements, the next time with psychedelic special effects. The records weren't selling.

When the Rolling Stones came to the U.S. for the first time in 1964, they wanted to record at Chess Records in Chicago because that was the studio where Muddy Waters worked. Keith Richards went there one day to meet his idol and found the great man painting the ceiling. Richards recalls that Waters was gracious but the look in his eye said, "Well, you can be painting the ceiling next year." Years later, Waters credited the Stones with reviving

his career in the late 1960s.

In the 1970s, Waters toured extensively, appearing in Europe, Japan, and Australia. He won several Grammy Awards and recorded with a bevy of rock stars. He also began a successful collaboration with Texas-born guitarist Johnny Winter, who produced his last albums. In 1977, Waters played the staff picnic at Jimmy Carter's White House. His last record, "King Bee," was recorded in 1981. Muddy Waters died in his sleep, of cancer, in his suburban Chicago home on April 30, 1983. He was sixty-eight years old.

Waters was a brilliant artist and a great entertainer. He left behind a huge body of recorded work, which stands on its own merits, but that is only part of the Muddy Waters legacy. Historically, he was a true link to the beginnings of the blues, and the generation of musicians he inspired, both white and black, carried his music to virtually every corner of the globe.

Perhaps more than anything else, Waters is important because he gave musicians of all races permission to go wherever the blues might take them. To him it was a living art form, not a historical artifact. As Keith Richards said in a 1993 interview, Muddy Waters "took everything from where he's growing up and living and hearing and projecting it and making it work for himself and then still growing with it. I mean, those guys never stopped growing."

MEMPHIS SLIM

P eter "Memphis Slim" Chatman was born into a famous musical family. His great-uncles were the Chatmon Brothers (some family members spelled it with an "a," others used an "o"), who also formed the core of the popular Mississippi Sheiks string band of the 1920s. When Chatman was fifteen, the Sheiks' song, "Sitting on Top of the World" (later a rock-and-roll hit for Cream), was one of the year's biggest-selling records.

But Peter Chatman wasn't interested in string-band music, guitars, mandolins, and such. He was born and raised in Memphis, and it was a piano town. National

Memphis Slim in Chicago, 1959. The night-club atmosphere was simulated for the photograph, but the smooth, urbane attitude was real.

The hands of the master, Memphis Slim, Chicago, 1959.

Prohibition was in effect, and most of Peter Chatman's childhood was spent in Memphis honky-tonks, where rollicking piano music accompanied the constant flow of bootleg liquor, gambling, and prostitution.

There were many such places up and down Beale Street where a piano player could find work, but no stool was more coveted than the one at the Midway Cafe, on the corner of Beale and Fourth Avenue. While still in his teens, Chatman became the piano player at the Midway, succeeding Roosevelt Sykes. The Midway was a nice place to work compared to most other saloons, but especially

compared to being outside in the park like a Memphis guitarist. Inside, where only piano players worked, the weather was much better and so were the tips, and the whiskey was more convenient.

Chatman gave up his privileged stool on Beale Street when the Memphis scene began to change after Prohibition. The rooms weren't as nice anymore, and the record companies had stopped sending field units south to record local talent. Now, toward the end of the 1930s, everything seemed to be happening in Chicago. Always ambitious, Pete Chatman moved there in 1939 and fell in with Roosevelt Sykes, who showed him around. Sykes, in his midthirties then, was well established on the Chicago blues scene. Chatman, a decade younger, appreciated his assistance.

Sykes also helped Chatman join the select group of musicians who produced the Bluebird library for Lester Melrose. A white businessman who also made many early jazz records, Melrose was the dominant force in the blues recording industry from 1928 until 1945. The Melrose system used the same core of musicians in both featured and backup roles. In other words, everyone played on everyone else's records. This was highly efficient and, more importantly, the record-buying public loved the product. Even though most postwar critics condemned Melrose for creating a homoge-

nous sound and tampering with "pure" country blues, his "Bluebird beat" dominated recorded blues throughout the Depression.

The musical, social, and spiritual center of the Chicago group was blues singer Big Bill Broonzy, who took a liking to the young piano player, now dubbed "Memphis Slim." Soon Slim was an integral part of the small, tight-knit community of artists and friends that included Broonzy, Sykes, Memphis Minnie, John Lee "Sonny Boy" Williamson (the first one), Arthur "Big Boy" Crudup, Tampa Red, Little Brother Montgomery, Jazz Gillum, Lonnie Johnson, Washboard Sam, Walter Davis, Big Joe Williams, and even "Georgia" Tom Dorsey, who later went on to create modern gospel music.

Memphis Slim mostly worked as an accompanist during this period, primarily with Broonzy. Sometime in the early 1940s, it was Broonzy, a close friend who was almost old enough to be Slim's father, who recommended that he "stop imitating Roosevelt Sykes" and form his own band. Slim took the advice and his group, Memphis Slim and the Houserockers, introduced a new sound to the Chicago blues. It was a seven-piece ensemble with guitar, bass, drums, piano, and something new—three saxophones, two tenors and an alto. Slim had the horns play the harmonica parts of traditional blues tunes, which gave the band "a big fat sound and a swinging tempo," as he would later describe it.

The Houserockers recorded successfully after the war and continued to be a local favorite until the end of the decade. Memphis Slim was the leader, pianist, and principal singer, and it was during this period that he also evolved into a gifted composer. The best known of his compositions, written during the Houserocker period, is "Every Day I Have the Blues," now a blues standard made famous by B. B. King.

Throughout the 1940s and into the 1950s, Slim was Broonzy's regular accompanist, the only one who could follow along as Broonzy got "into his blues." When black audiences turned away with the advent of rock and roll, Broonzy started to perform in Europe and Slim went along. He made regular

Chicago, 1959.

tours of Europe, both before and after Broonzy's death in 1958, and finally settled there for good in the early 1960s. He married a young Frenchwoman, lived in Paris, played in prestigious clubs, recorded several successful albums, and became quite wealthy.

Memphis Slim often spoke bitterly about the United States and the treatment he and other African-American blues musicians received here, both in his native South and the urban North. He was especially disgusted by the fate of Joe McCoy, Memphis Minnie's first husband. McCoy had written the song, "Why Don't You Do Right?," which later

became a big hit for Peggy Lee. While his body lay in a South Side funeral home on a cold Chicago night in 1950, Peggy Lee was downtown at the Chicago Theater, making big money singing the dead man's song, yet Joe McCoy died so poor that Memphis Slim and his other friends had to take up a collection to bury him.

As Memphis Slim reflected on the incident years later, rich and content in his Paris home, he knew he had no desire ever to live in the United States again, although he did make periodic appearances throughout the 1970s. Sick during most of the 1980s, he died in Paris in 1988. He is buried in Memphis.

JOHN LEE HOOKER

The great minimalist of the blues, John Lee Hooker thinks and talks the way he plays: simple, direct, with no notes wasted. "The blues is the only music," he told a *People* interviewer in 1990. "Everything else they're doing—rock 'n' roll, pop—it all comes from there. Something about a woman. Something about a man. Something about a man and a woman. That's the blues. I don't try to figure it out too much, though. Just is."

Staying with that simple formula—and Hooker has kept his music simple, too, generally preferring solo voice, guitar, and foot stomping to big production numbers—John Lee Hooker has worked its infinite variations like no one else. He may be the most recorded bluesman in history, with more than five hundred tracks and dozens of albums to his credit. Between new recordings and reissues, fans today usually have four or five new John Lee Hooker albums to choose from every year.

John Lee Hooker is also, at age

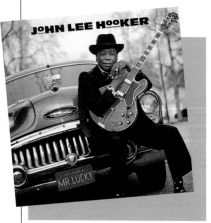

Interview session, 1964.

seventy-eight, one of the few bluesmen who has lived long enough to reap the rewards of his work. "I got this big mansion in Long Beach," he told a *Newsweek* interviewer on the occasion of his 1995 release, "Chill Out." "I got chauffeurs. I got a long stretch black limousine. Bar in it. VCRs, telephone, everything. I got a suit for every day of the week." On recordings and in concert appearances in the 1980s and 1990s, Hooker has shared the spotlight with Bonnie Raitt, Carlos Santana, Johnny Winter, B. B. King, Buddy Guy, Keith Richards, Branford Marsalis, Etta James, Koko Taylor, Ry Cooder, Robert Cray, Booker T. Jones, Joe Cocker, Gregg Allman, Johnnie Johnson, Albert Collins, John Hammond, Van Morrison, and other rock, jazz, and blues stars. Not bad for a man who was still sweeping floors in a Detroit Chrysler plant when he was thirty-four.

John Lee Hooker was born in 1917 in Clarksdale, Mississippi, the legendary epicenter of the Delta blues. In his own family and at a very young age, he experienced the classic sacred/sacrilegious dichotomy so common in the lives of blues musicians. His father was a Baptist minister, and no blues was ever played in Reverend Hooker's household, only sacred songs or spirituals.

When Hooker was still a boy, his parents separated and his mother married William Moore, a farmer and occasional bluesman. The union was especially good for Minnie Moore's fourth child, because Will Moore adopted John Lee and taught the child everything he knew about blues guitar. "I used to hear my stepfather, when I was a kid. My style, I got it from him," said Hooker in a 1993 interview. "Everything I do is direct from Will Moore, my stepfather. He played just like I'm playing today. I learned from him. He played that kind of stuff—foot stomping." Today the style is uniquely Hooker's, and as original and distinctive as any in music. There is only one John Lee Hooker.

When he was about twelve, Hooker started performing with Moore at fish fries, country suppers, and dances around the Clarksdale area. Another local boy about Hooker's age who was getting started the same way was Muddy Waters. Hooker listened to records by Lonnie Johnson and Texan Blind Lemon Jefferson, but his idol was another Texan, Aaron Thibeaux "T-Bone" Walker. All three were guitarists, but Jefferson and Johnson were already men in their thirties when Hooker started to play. Walker was barely twenty but already recording and touring. Hooker remembers that he used to follow Walker around "like a little puppy following his mama."

At age fourteen, Hooker tried to join the army. He spent three months stationed in Detroit before they figured out how young he was and sent him home, but he didn't stay there long. His first move was to Memphis, then Cincinnati, and finally back to Detroit, but it took him more than ten years. He was twenty-six years old.

As he had in Memphis and Cincinnati, Hooker worked both in and out of music in Detroit. His first record, made five years after his arrival, was also his first hit: "Boogie Chillen." His fame continued to grow, though slowly, and he wasn't able to leave the broom at Chrysler until 1951. That year his "I'm in the Mood" sold a million copies.

Hooker never swept floors again, but many fans believe his early career was inhibited by his remaining in Detroit, where audiences were smaller and recording studios were cruder than in nearby Chicago. Although he recorded constantly, the next big hit didn't come until "Boom Boom" in 1961. Soon after that, he entered an acoustic phase, playing folk clubs, festivals, and college campuses throughout the United States and Europe for predominantly white audiences.

As a result of that wide exposure, he became an idol to thousands of aspiring young guitarists on both sides of the Atlantic. John Lee Hooker was one of the first Delta bluesmen to record with an English rock band, in 1965, but his choice was inauspicious. Does anyone remember the Groundhogs? Other Hooker disciples did better, including Ike Turner, Jimi Hendrix, Eric Clapton, Jeff Beck, and Jimmy Page. He also inspired American blues rockers like Canned Heat, Johnny Winter, and Buddy Guy. The first big ZZ Top hit, "LaGrange" (1973), borrowed heavily from Hooker, especially from "Boom Boom." Since the midseventies, Bonnie Raitt has been his most persistent booster.

In 1968 and '69, Hooker won major music awards in Europe and the United States. In the seventies, he appeared on popular TV shows like "Midnight Special" and "Don Kirshner's Rock Concert." His 1990 duet with Bonnie Raitt won a Grammy. His nineties albums, "The Healer" and "Mr. Lucky," were million sellers.

John Lee Hooker's deep, almost-droning voice is his trademark. If Son House and Robert Johnson epitomize rage in the blues, Hooker has the corner on sheer, terrifying despair. His is the voice of doom, announced and answered by moaning guitar runs and stalked by his relentlessly tapping foot. Unlike many longtime survivors in the music business, Hooker has never altered his style. As B. B. King said in a 1993 joint interview, "When John Lee Hooker plays, it's like writing his name."

Interview session, 1964.

JIMMY REED

Jimmy Reed was a Chicago bluesman from Mississippi whose records sold like hotcakes in Texas. He was discovered by and spent the best years of his career with a record company that began in Gary, Indiana, a company that almost became the first major black-owned record producer in the United States, before Motown. Jimmy Reed's career was also made possible by the two people closest to him. One was Eddie Taylor, his guitarist, musical collaborator, and childhood friend. The other was his wife, Mary Lee Reed, whom he called "Mama" and who wrote

Jimmy Reed in concert at Chicago's Trianon Ballroom in the mid-1960s.

or cowrote most of his songs.

The record company to which Reed's fate was so closely linked was VJ or Vee Jay. The "V" stood for Vivian Carter, and the "J" was her husband, Jimmy Bracken. In 1948, the couple opened a record shop in Gary, Indiana, then a booming, steel-making metropolis about forty miles southeast of Chicago. Vivian was a popular disc jockey on a local radio station. In 1952, along with Vivian's brother, Calvin Carter, they started a record company to compete with Chess, then the unrivaled leader in the Chicago market. When the company got going they moved the offices from Gary into Chicago. Eventually Vee Jay signed Jimmy Reed, John Lee Hooker, and Jerry Butler. They also had the Dells, the Four Seasons, Gladys Knight and the Pips, and the first U.S. distribution of four singles by a new English group called the Beatles. (That was a fluke. Capitol Records soon came to its senses and exercised its option to distribute the group's records in the United States.)

Like John Lee Hooker, Reed was a great blues minimalist. His songs were simple and languid, with Eddie Taylor playing essentially the same slow guitar boogie on every track, punctuated by Reed's harp. The songs were mesmerizing. More than anything else, they were very danceable, which was the secret of their success.

Jimmy Reed was born Mathis James Reed in 1925 in Washington County, Mississippi, not far from the home of B. B. King, who was born the same year. Reed played around with guitars as a child, and his father taught him how to play harmonica when he was about seven. One of his friends at that time was Eddie Taylor, but they drifted apart. As a teenager, Reed left home and moved to Chicago, working odd jobs. When World War II began he was drafted and served in the navy for five years. Returning to the Midwest after the war, he worked in a Gary steel foundry during the week and played blues in Chicago whenever he could. In 1950, he ran into Taylor, who had become an accomplished guitarist (much better than Reed), and they began their partnership.

Reed signed with Vee Jay in 1953. The audition was actually Eddie Taylor's, and Reed just went along to accompany him, but Vee Jay liked the combination of Reed on vocals and harmonica and Taylor on guitar. The hit parade began in 1955 with "You Don't Have to Go." Between 1953 and 1966, Jimmy Reed was as big as B. B. King and bigger than Muddy Waters, Howlin' Wolf and Little Walter. In all, Reed had twenty-two chart singles in thirteen years. Many of these songs, all written by Mr. and Mrs. Reed, became standards and hits for others, including "Big Boss Man," "Bright Lights, Big City," and "Ain't That Lovin' You, Baby?"

Many Vee Jay acts, including Jimmy Reed, were popular with young record buyers of both races, another new phenomenon in the late fifties and early sixties. Nowhere was Reed more popular than in Texas, where he inspired a whole generation of "swamp blues" bands. Vee Jay looked like a great success story, but then, suddenly in 1965, it was over. Jimmy Reed's career never recovered, but it was already in trouble. In 1957, Reed had learned that he had epilepsy, but instead of stopping some of his more unhealthy habits, he had increased them. He was constantly drunk, missing gigs and burning friends. By the mid sixties, Eddie Taylor had had enough, and Mama also left. In 1965, the only recording home Reed had ever known, Vee Jay, went bankrupt.

Reed had one more hit, "Knockin' at Your Door," in 1966. Thereafter, he was often too drunk at shows to complete a set. He died in 1976.

Along with Muddy Waters, Buddy Guy, B. B. King, and Freddie King, Jimmy Reed was very influential on the early work of English blues rockers like the Animals, the Rolling Stones, the Moody Blues, and the Spencer Davis Group. In the United States, his songs have been favored by country and country/rock artists.

B.B. KING

A summary of B. B. King's career demands superlatives: Best Known, Best Selling, Most Recorded, Most Acclaimed, Most Widely Traveled, Most Successful, Hardest Working, Most Imitated, Best Loved. For almost fifty years, this musical legend's career has never once faltered or even plateaued. He just keeps getting bigger and bigger. He has won five Grammys, has more than 125 albums out, and his name is synonymous with the blues to audiences all over the world.

King has also had a pervasive influence on other guitarists. He was the original guitar hero and more than any other artist is responsible for the style of fast, clean, single-string solo playing used by virtually every guitarist today, whether in blues, jazz, rock, or country. A person can't turn on the radio without becoming aware of the massive effect B. B. King has had on popular music.

In the context of blues music, one way to think of B. B. King is as the first modern bluesman. Before him, every bluesman learned his craft through an informal apprenticeship. By hanging around, watching, listening, and playing with local masters, these early musicians gradually picked things up. Traveling shows and, later, phonograph records were influential, too, and talented individuals have always innovated, but mostly blues musicians played like other local players did. When they started working, they performed in the same joints where they had learned to play, with their family and neighbors who knew them and knew where they came from as their audience. Even Muddy

B. B. King performing at Chicago's Trianon Ballroom in 1963.

Waters and John Lee Hooker, just a decade older than B. B. King, grew up this way.

For King and most blues artists who followed him, it was different. King's early playing was influenced more by sounds he heard on records and radio than by live performers. The musical influences he chose to listen to and absorb were incredibly diverse, ranging from Lonnie Johnson to Django Reinhardt. Everything anybody was doing on a guitar caught his ear.

The audiences he played for were different, too. In deference to his family, who were mostly religious and opposed to the blues, he didn't play where he lived. From the beginning, every audience was a crowd of strangers to be wooed and won. He wanted to please them because he wanted to come back, but he always hungered to play in new towns, bigger towns. Because he played for so many new audiences, he developed a knack for quickly gauging out the mood of a crowd, so he could tailor the rest of his show accordingly.

King kept touring further and further from home because he didn't want to be like the bluesmen who cycled around the local juke joints. He preferred to be like

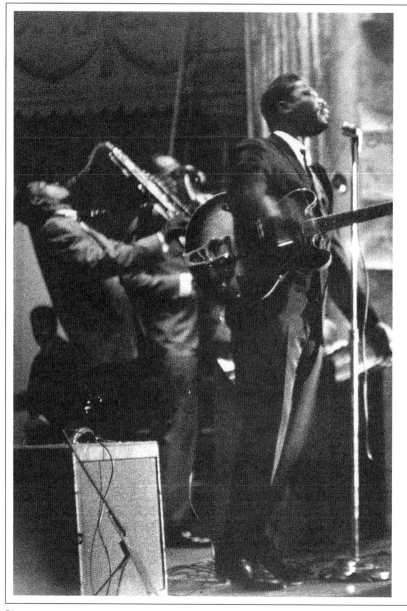

the people on the radio, like Lonnie Johnson and T-Bone Walker, or for that matter, Jimmie Rodgers and Hank Williams. He chose to be like the people he saw on the "soundies": special juke-boxes that played short films of Ella Fitzgerald, Nat "King" Cole, and Cab Calloway. Or like Sonny Boy Williamson (the second one) and Robert "Junior" Lockwood, who were both on the radio and came down to Indianola on week-ends to play at Johnny Jones's Nightclub. Or Louis Jordan, who also performed there.

Riley Ben King wanted to be like all of them.

He was born in 1925 on a plan-tation near Indianola, Mississippi. When he was four, his parents separated, and he moved with his mother about sixty miles east to another farm near Kilmichael. She died there when he was only nine, and for the next five years, he worked as a farmhand for the family that had employed her. He plowed in the spring, hoed all summer, and picked cotton in the fall.

When he was fourteen, King's father found him and moved him back to Indianola, where his new family introduced him to guitars. One aunt was married to a minis-ter who played guitar and let the boy practice with it on Sunday afternoons. Another, younger aunt let him listen to her Blind Lemon Jefferson and Lonnie Johnson records. Soon he had a guitar, was learning how to play it, and had formed a gospel quartet to perform in area churches. In 1943, with World War II in its second year, the eighteen-year-old King did a brief tour in the army. There he was exposed to jazz: Charlie Christian in Benny Goodman's band, and the three-fingered French gypsy genius, Django Reinhardt. While at Fort Benning, Georgia, he also started playing the blues.

In and out of the army in less than a year, King returned to Indianola and gospel music, but the blues soon drew him to Memphis. Once the war was over, he gave the city a try, playing in the parks around Beale Street for tips, often with his cousin, Booker T. Washington White, with whom he also lived. Cousin Bukka White had had a pretty good blues career himself

B. B. King performing at Chicago's Trianon Ballroom in 1963.

before and during the war, despite spending two years in Parchman Farm Prison. He had recorded, toured the Midwest and South, and entertained the troops, but now he was back in Memphis, only forty years old and not doing much of anything. Young Riley King wanted more than that, but he couldn't seem to get going, so he returned to Indianola briefly before trying Memphis again in 1948.

On the second trip, the first thing he did was approach Sonny Boy Williamson about appearing on his radio show. This was the same Sonny Boy

(really Alex Miller) who had performed in Indianola and had once been married to Howlin' Wolf's sister. King's appearance on Williamson's radio show led to a regular gig at Miss Annie's, a casino and tavern in West Memphis, Arkansas, but that job was dependent on King obtaining a regular radio show of his own.

He approached WDIA in Memphis, the first all-black radio station in the United States. He had been entering station-sponsored talent contests and had won enough of them to finally get an audition. Soon he was on the air, competing directly with Williamson, whose sponsor,

Hadacol, was a brand of patent medicine. King's sponsor was a rival concoction, Peptikon, and his first musical hit was the four-line Peptikon jingle, which went like this: "Peptikon, it sure is good. Peptikon, it sure is good. Peptikon, it sure is good. You can get it anywhere in your neighborhood." Somehow the twenty-three-year-old singer with the baby face and sweet guitar made it memorable, and he became a local celebrity. He made personal appearances for Peptikon and gobbled up longer and longer blocks of daily airtime on WDIA, both as a performer and a disc jockey.

King stayed at the station for four years, until 1953. During that time, he toured as often and as far as he could, until in the later years the station often had to "re-create" his radio show from a collection of acetate disks from previous broadcasts. These "best of" shows were made to sound live, and King briefly lost his sponsor when it was discovered that they were sometimes prerecorded. By the time he left WDIA, after his hit with "Three O'Clock Blues," King was performing about three hundred shows a year, a pace he has continued ever since.

B. B. King cites Lonnie Johnson as one of his earliest and biggest influences. In his heyday, when King was still a boy, Johnson recorded constantly and toured widely. He wrote, sang, and played the blues but is best known for his guitar solos, which defy easy categorization. He played many kinds of music—anything to please an audience—and performed with everybody important, including Duke Ellington, Louis Armstrong, and Bessie Smith. He was everything the boy who became B. B. King wanted to be.

But in the 1950s, while King was a young man on his way up, he watched the great Lonnie Johnson slide all the way down to a janitor's broom. The old man still had one more comeback ahead of him, but Lonnie Johnson's fall may explain some of B. B. King's relentless drive. No matter how big, how successful he becomes, there is always one more encore, one more show, one more town, one more audience to please, and he will do whatever it takes to make people happy. During the 1950s and most of the 1960s, B. B. King was one of the biggest stars in black America, but he was virtually unknown to white Americans. He worked the "chitlin circuit" of one-night stands before all-black audiences in countless auditoriums and dance halls, mostly in the South. Always he was looking for someplace new to play, where he could test himself before an audience that had never heard him before. Because he was always on the road, he rarely saw either of his wives or any of the other women who bore and raised his thirteen children, but he supported all of them financially.

In 1969, B. B. King scored his biggest hit, breaking through the color barrier and into the mainstream for good. The song was a beautiful blues ballad in a minor key, "The Thrill Is Gone," first recorded by Roy Hawkins in 1951. It got B. B. King the first of his many appearances on Johnny Carson's "Tonight Show," and he toured with Ike and Tina Turner and the Rolling Stones. The next year, he recorded an album that became an early seventies icon and made him the darling of FM radio, "B. B. King Live in Cook County Jail."

Things have been pretty much like that ever since: touring, records, TV, the whole superstar whirl. In recent years, King has been showered with honors: a Grammy Lifetime Achievement Award in 1987, the Presidential Medal of Freedom and a star on Hollywood's Walk of Fame in 1990. He opened his second B. B. King Blues Club in 1994 in Los Angeles, after launching the original on Beale Street in Memphis. Los Angeles is another city B. B. King has called home, not that it matters where he technically resides at any given moment. He still travels most of the time even though he now lives in Las Vegas, one of the few places on earth where a performer of his stature can work all year.

If there is any concern about the King of the Blues, it is that he has

B. B. King performing at Chicago's Trianon Ballroom in 1963.

entered his seventh decade without an apparent heir. The late Stevie Ray Vaughn may have been it, or maybe Eric Clapton will add "King of the Blues" to his other crowns. Buddy Guy, though qualified for the job, is only a decade younger than King, who shows no signs of slowing down. Robert Cray, born the year King left WDIA, is the likeliest candidate of his generation.

B. B. King cares about his legacy and worries that future generations of African-American children won't learn enough about the blues and the way black people have changed the course of popular music. In the seventies, he complained that "our young people think the blues is low-down and obscene." Young blacks should be proud of the blues, he said, "because that's the one thing Negroes have that nobody in the world can equal. Nobody can do the blues like black people do the blues." In 1992, he told an *Ebony* magazine reporter that "to be a black person and sing the blues, you are black twice" because blues songs reflect so much of black history. Whatever the future remembers, no one will ever say that B. B. King did not do everything in his power to keep blues music alive.

LITTLE WALTER

Like Muddy Waters, who had arrived a few years earlier, Little Walter Jacobs bridged two eras in Chicago blues history after he reached the big city in the mid-1940s. Like Waters, he was "sponsored" into the inner circle of Chicago blues musicians by Big Bill Broonzy, godfather of the group, and Tampa Red, an equally venerable figure.

Little Walter Jacobs was about fifteen or sixteen years old when he was discovered playing for handouts on Maxwell Street. Already he was a better-than-average guitar player and a fine singer, but what really set him apart was his harp playing.

A concert performance in 1966, Little Walter sharing the bill with Otis Rush and Buddy Guy.

From the beginning, it was clear that he would rival John Lee "Sonny Boy" Williamson, then the reigning king of the Chicago harmonica. Before he was finished, Little Walter would not only surpass that Sonny Boy and the second one (Rice Miller), along with everyone else, but would also come to define blues harmonica, just as B. B. King would later define blues guitar.

To most of the people who remember him from his heyday in the 1950s, Little Walter was the quintessential tough street punk, a little bully—cocky, strutting, paranoid, and quick with an insult, nasty remark, dig, or cut; sometimes he was also quick with a knife or pistol. Born in 1930 on a farm near Alexandria, Louisiana, he grew up poor and did what he had to do to survive, playing harmonica and begging pennies on the street from the age of eight. At twelve, he hit the road, stopping first in New Orleans, then settling into a steady gig in Monroe, in the northern part of the state. He was a small, skinny thirteen-year-old who sang, danced, and played pretty good harp.

For the next two or three years, he worked in the area around Memphis, where he became acquainted with Robert "Junior" Lockwood, already a veteran bluesman, and learned how to play guitar. He also spent a few months in St. Louis. Sometime

around age fifteen or sixteen he made it to Chicago, where he hit the streets, joining the large and ever-changing tribe of musicians who set up each day and played for whatever they could get on the side streets around the Maxwell Street Market.

For many generations, Chicago's Maxwell Street was the place where all new arrivals eventually came, not just African-Americans from the South, but hordes of other soon-to-be-hyphenated Americans arriving from Europe and Asia as well. Maxwell Street was an outdoor market where literally anything was for sale. It was located in a neighborhood where inexpensive housing could be found, and shops and ser-

vices that also catered to the poor and newly arrived were located. Today it is gone, gobbled up by the expanding campus of the University of Illinois at Chicago, but in the 1940s it was the Schwab's Drugstore of the

blues, where all newcomers came to be discovered.

Little Walter Jacobs was discovered there by the Broonzy crowd just as their long reign was drawing to a close. His first break came when a tiny, short-lived record company on Maxwell Street recorded him in 1947. These records got him other work with musicians in the Broonzy circle. In 1948, Sonny Boy Williamson stopped an ice pick with his skull, and a lot more work started to flow Little Walter's way. That same year, Muddy Waters made his first hit record and suddenly became the hottest thing in Chicago. Within two years, Little Walter would join the Muddy Waters Band.

This was the legendary Muddy Waters Band of the early 1950s, consisting of Waters on guitar and vocals, Little Walter on harp, Jimmy Rogers on guitar, and "Baby Face" Leroy Foster on drums. The Muddy Waters Band made magic and was the toast of the town, playing in all the best clubs and lounges.

In the show clubs and lounges, and on the road in dance halls, blues bands usually began their sets with a signature opening song. It was typically an up-tempo song, played by the sidemen, designed to get the audience excited and screaming in anticipation of the headliner's arrival. Often it wasn't really a song, just a continuous groove. It might not even have a name. In 1952, at the request of their fans, the Muddy Waters Band recorded their show opener. It was an instrumental showpiece for Little Walter's harp, and Leonard Chess, president of Chess Records, named it "Juke." It became one of the biggest hits of that year, shooting to number one on the rhythm-and-blues charts and staying on the list for sixteen weeks.

With the success of "Juke," Little Walter couldn't wait to start his solo career. He was so anxious that he ran out on the band while they were touring when he noticed the patrons in a Shreveport, Louisiana, dance hall playing "Juke" over and over again on the jukebox. Muddy Waters and Little Walter seldom appeared together in live performances after that, but Little Walter continued to record as a sideman for Waters. Together in the studio, they created some of the greatest blues recordings ever made.

Back in Chicago, Little Walter hired a band that had been working behind another young harpist, Junior Wells. Forty-two years later, in an interview with *Guitar Player* magazine, Wells said that those were still his favorite sidemen of all time. Fortunately for Wells, he got the best consolation prize of all time: Little Walter's job with Muddy Waters.

Little Walter's career took off like a rocket after that, and he and Muddy Waters dominated the rhythm-and-blues charts through 1954. For the rest of the decade, he had a charted hit every year except 1957. In 1955, he went to number one again with "My Babe," a Willie Dixon creation based on the old gospel song, "This Train." Dixon wrote it for Little Walter in 1953 but couldn't persuade him to record it until two years later. Dixon was right about "My Babe." It was perfect for Little Walter, a light, bouncy number that made good use of his smooth, pop vocal style, modeled after T-Bone Walker. It was also perfect in concert, letting Little Walter strut around on stage and flirt with the women as he sang. He needed those light vocal numbers in the show to give him a break from his ferocious and exhausting harp blowing.

Later in the decade, even though he had some chart success, bad habits began catching up with Little Walter, and his star started to fade. In the 1960s, things got even worse. He sank deeper and deeper into his drinking. Never too likable in the best of times, he now became sullen and bitter. He and Rice Miller, the second Sonny Boy Williamson, feuded constantly.

Miller, also a harp player and twenty years older than Little Walter, loved to bait him. By 1968, Little Walter was still playing in clubs around Chicago, but his career was going nowhere. In February, he got into a fight in the street, got home and into bed, but died of his injuries while he slept. He was thirty-seven.

Many commentators assert that Little Walter was the best blues harpist ever. Almost everyone will rank him in their top five. Most also agree that he, more than any other harp player, defined the way that amplified harp should be played in an electric blues band.

FREDDIE KING

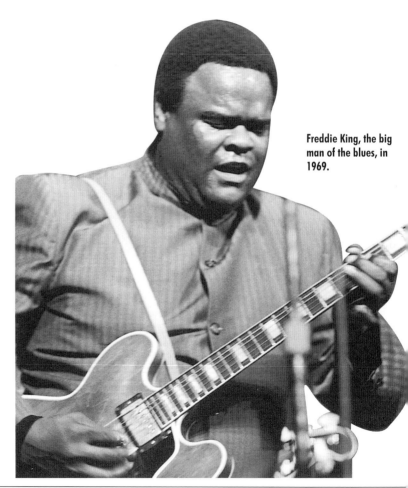

T here were giants in Chicago after World War II. The blues became bigger, more confident, more potent, more muscular, more powerful. The optimism of America in that era, right after the war, was unprecedented and has not been matched since. Almost all Americans, black and white, believed the future was going to be better than the past. The Depression was over, Prohibition was over, Hitler was dead. We had WON, damn it. We had kicked ASS. The rest of the world, allies and enemies alike, was on its back. America was still on its feet, the only one left standing after the biggest bar brawl in history.

This macho sense of power, of virility, of invincibility suffused American culture, including the blues. African-Americans realized

Freddie King, the big man of the blues, in 1969.

sooner than most how little had really changed, and they were the first to be laid off when the go-go economy slowed down, but for a brief time, especially in the cities and nowhere more than Chicago, folks had a few dollars in their pockets and were ready to rock the house.

In the Chicago blues clubs, guitars and basses were now amplified, drum kits got bigger, sound systems got better, and everything got louder. In this era of bigger, faster, and better, guitarists were the heaviest giants in town. They all walked the earth back then: Muddy Waters, of course, but also Earl Hooker, Matt "Guitar" Murphy, Magic Sam Maghett, Hubert Sumlin, Luther Allison, Hound Dog Taylor, Jimmy Rogers, Eddie Taylor, Robert "Junior" Lockwood, Otis Rush, and Buddy Guy. Among these men, giants all, no one was big-

Dressed for the times in 1969.

ger, literally, than Freddie King.

At six-feet, seven-inches tall and carrying about three hundred pounds, King could have played football. Instead, he played guitar, but with comparable force. His fast-draw, gunslinger style betrayed his Texas heritage, even though his music was mostly Chicago bred. He made the lead guitar the star like no one had before and charted with something almost unheard of, the blues instrumental. He also excelled at the virtual instrumental, in which words are merely vocal sounds, lacking the content of a real blues lyric. "Goin' Down," a song written

for him by Memphis songwriter Don Nix, is today a staple for every blues-based bar band in Chicago (and everywhere else).

Freddy King switched the spelling of his name to "Freddie" toward the end of his career for no apparent reason. He is also not related to any of the other famous bluesmen named King. He was born in 1934 in the same East Texas countryside that had produced T-Bone Walker a quarter century earlier. Like Walker, King's mother got him his first guitar and taught him how to play when he was a small boy, and he learned the country blues of his family and neighbors. On records, his people preferred the country approach of

Lightnin' Hopkins to the "jump blues" of Walker, though King gravitated more to Walker. He also liked Lonnie Johnson and, later, Elmore James and the "other" King, B. B.

When he was fifteen, King moved with his mother to Chicago. He quickly became enamored of the local music scene and started sitting in whenever he could. He played with various bands, then formed his own when he was seventeen. The cofounder of his Every Hour's Blues Boys band had just been released from prison. The other guy's guitar was in the pawnshop and he didn't own an amp. They redeemed the axe, both plugged into King's box, and played their first gig. That band lasted about a year; then they joined Little Sonny Cooper, who needed two guitarists because he played harmonica.

King cut some records with Cooper's band, then got his own chance to record as a singer in 1956. On these records, he did not play guitar, a task that fell to Robert "Junior" Lockwood, a veteran Chicago musician who had learned his blues in the Delta from his stepfather, Robert Johnson. These first records, on a small and struggling label, were moderately successful, but they led to a long-term recording deal with a bigger company, King Records, based in Cincinnati.

King's first release for King Records (actually he recorded on their Federal subsidiary) was also his first hit, "You've Got to Love Her with a Feeling." Others followed. The song that became his trademark, "Hideaway," began his successful string of instrumentals. "San-Ho-Zay," "Sen-Sa-Shun," "The Stumble," and "Remington Ride" came later. His record company's formula was to release each Freddie King single with a vocal on the A side and an instrumental on the back; often the instrumental was the bigger hit. Albums were assembled the same way, one with vocals, another without, and were released within a few months of each other.

Although King and his long-time pianist, Sonny Thompson, are credited with writing "Hideaway," they may only have named it. King either learned the song from Hound Dog Taylor or Magic Sam Maghett, or they all learned it from Irving Spencer, who actually wrote it, according to Willie Dixon, who knew them all. The song was named after the place where King played in those days, Mel's Hideaway Lounge on Chicago's West Side. The parentage of "You've Got to Love Her with a Feeling" is similarly shaky. It is credited to King on his records but is clearly the same song as "Love with a Feeling," recorded by Tampa Red in 1938. King and Thompson also claimed authorship for their version of the blues standard, "See See Rider," renamed "C.C. Baby."

King's career got a second wind in the late 1960s when he hooked up with the popular blues/rock singer, Leon Russell. At Russell's shows, King played the opening set, then Russell and his backup singers joined the band, and King played through Russell's set as well. King also recorded on Russell's Shelter label during its short life and produced his final albums for Polydor.

On Christmas Day, 1976, Freddie King performed in Dallas, not far from his boyhood home. Three days later, he died of heart failure complicated by bleeding stomach ulcers. He was forty-two years old.

Many Freddie King songs have become classics, and his versions of many blues standards are considered the definitive interpretations. Everybody still plays his "Goin' Down" and "Palace of the King," and his "I'm Tore Down" is on Eric Clapton's 1994 "From the Cradle," the first all-blues album ever to debut at number one on the *Billboard* chart. According to guitarist Jimmie Vaughn, a Texas band in the 1960s couldn't get off the stage without playing "Hideaway" at least once. Listen to King's 1975 "Larger Than Life" live album, then go into any blues bar on earth. It's the same music. That's the sound of a big, happy, optimistic Chicago in the late 1950s and early 1960s. That's the sound of Freddie King.

OTIS RUSH

The life of a bluesman has always been hard. It was brutally hard in "Jim Crow" Mississippi in the early decades of the century, but times have been frustrating and unrewarding for many contemporary bluesmen, too, even those with an abundance of talent and credentials. Consider the case of Otis Rush.

The Chicago-based guitarist and singer exploded on the scene in 1956. Rush was just twenty-two years old, and he had been playing guitar for only two years when the ubiquitous Willie Dixon heard him perform and asked Rush to record one of Dixon's songs for a new label called Cobra. Dixon produced the session and played bass. "I Can't Quit You, Baby"

A concert performance in 1966, sharing the bill with Buddy Guy and Little Walter.

was Rush's first record and one of the first for Cobra, too. For both, it was also their biggest hit, peaking at number six on *Billboard's* rhythm-and-blues chart as 1956 drew to a close.

It is a sad truth in the music business that musicians never make money from their first hits, so when it is also their biggest hit, they've got trouble. Trouble followed Otis Rush. Over the next two years, he and Dixon made some of the best blues records of the postwar era, but they were hampered by appearing on a small, independent label with an eccentric owner, who was a gambler, con man, and mobster wanna-be. Cobra Records was never more than a room behind a record shop on Roosevelt Road, held together by Dixon's talent and determination to succeed following his split with Chess Records. Rush, who had tried

Otis Rush performing at the legendary Pepper's Lounge in 1963.

unsuccessfully to record for Chess, went along for the ride. After their initial success, Dixon took Rush to Florida for a tour and on the way, they were arrested six times for speeding. If that was an omen of things to come, no one recognized it at the time.

The body of Cobra's owner was hauled out of Lake ·Michigan one day in 1959. The record label promptly folded, and Dixon and Rush found themselves back at Chess. Dixon thrived, writing and producing a string of Howlin' Wolf hits, but Rush languished, eclipsed by his good friend Buddy Guy. He eventu-

ally signed with another small label, Houston-based Duke, but they tied him up for five years and only released one single.

The next deal, as the 1960s ended, was supposed to be the big one with a big-time label, Capitol Records. Instead, Capitol decided to quit the blues while Rush was still in the studio. The master tapes of that album, appropriately titled "Right Place, Wrong Time," sat on the shelf for five years. Finally released in 1976 on the Bullfrog label, the record earned critical raves and received a Grammy nomination.

Rush seemed star-crossed. By the late 1970s, the 1956–58 Cobra sessions had been declared bona fide classics, and nothing new Rush produced seemed to measure up. Even positive reviews of his later work inevitably contained the caveat, "though not as inspired as his Cobra sides." Trying to recapture that glory, he kept rerecording the early songs. Every album, it seemed, contained a new version of "I Can't Quit You, Baby," a song that was eventually appropriated by Led Zeppelin.

For Otis Rush, the last straw fell when Alligator Records acquired the U.S. rights to "Troubles Troubles," an album he had recorded in Sweden. Over his objections, Alligator decided to add keyboard to the tracks when it released the collection as "Lost in the Blues." It would be nearly twenty years before Rush entered a studio again.

In 1994, the same California production team that had engineered Buddy Guy's hugely successful 1990s' recordings tried to work the same magic for Otis Rush. The CD, "Ain't Enough Comin' In," contains versions of tunes by B. B. King, Albert King, Ray Charles, Sam Cooke, and Percy Mayfield. Both Rush's voice and guitar are in fine form on the set, and in interviews surrounding the release, Rush—now in his early sixties—seemed pleased with both the record and the company (Mercury) that released it. In live performances these days, Rush can range from

awesome to unfocused, but his skills are undiminished. It is still a pleasure to watch him work, especially in the intimate Chicago clubs where he usually performs.

Otis Rush was born in Philadelphia, Mississippi, in 1934. He played some harmonica as a boy but never considered a career in music. He thought of himself as a farmer. In 1954, he came to Chicago to visit his sister and she took him to hear Muddy Waters play at the Zanzibar. That was all it took. Rush immediately bought a guitar and started practicing day and night. Although Waters supplied the spark, the musician who most inspired Rush's music was B. B. King, whose guitar style borrowed as much from jazz as it did from traditional blues. Jazz gui-

tarist Kenny Burrell was another influence.

Part of the Otis Rush sound results from the fact that he is left-handed. Most left-handed guitarists restring their instruments so the low strings are on top and the high ones are on the bottom, just as they are for a right-handed player. The chords are then mirrored, but the fingering is essentially the same. So is the strumming and picking pattern. With the guitar restrung, a left-handed player shouldn't sound any different than a right-hander. Rush, however, took a different approach. He simply turned the guitar upside down and learned to play everything backward. A constant string bender, Rush pulls rather than pushing, which creates a slightly different sound.

Another early Rush innovation was the electric bass, which came along many years after electrified guitar. Willie Dixon played stand-up acoustic bass on Rush's Cobra recordings, but Rush never really liked that sound. He wanted something with an electric edge. Willie Warren, the second guitarist in Rush's band, tried a trick he remembered from down south. He tuned his top strings down an octave, cranked the bass on his amp, and played bass lines instead of chords.

The electric bass sound was an instant hit with audiences and other Chicago musicians. When he heard that Ike Turner had a Fender electric bass in his St. Louis band, Rush hurried down to check it out. Rush and Warren introduced the Fender electric bass to Chicago, and soon just about everyone was using it.

Although Rush created new instrumental sounds by using techniques borrowed from jazz and other sources, he was blessed with a pure blues voice. His vocal style is often compared to Robert Johnson's. At his best, Rush's singing is taut, anxious, tortured, and frighteningly close to despair.

Rush is usually classified as part of the "West Side school" of guitarists, a characterization he resents in part because he has always lived on Chicago's South Side. The label has stuck because Rush and fellow guitarists Buddy Guy and Magic Sam Maghett all have similar styles and all started out at

Otis Rush performing at the legendary Pepper's Lounge in 1963.

Cobra, which was located on the West Side. One of the characteristics of the West Side sound is the use of fast, heavy chording, a style that evolved because Rush heard horns in his head but couldn't afford to use them in his band. He substituted heavy chords on the guitar. Whether the other West Siders were thinking about horns, too, or just thinking about sounding like Otis Rush, we can't be sure.

You can hear an example of this technique on the original recording of "Double Trouble." There is saxophone on the track, but Rush's guitar plays all over it, and you can hear the

way he made up for its absence in live performances, when he could only afford a four-piece band. On the record, the sax is almost superfluous.

"Double Trouble" is an Otis Rush composition. Stevie Ray Vaughn covered it with great success and even gave the name to his band. The lyrics say a lot about the way Rush saw his life back then and, perhaps, still sees it: "I lay awake at nights, false love, just so troubled. It's hard to keep a job, laid off, having double trouble. Hey, hey, yeah; they say you can make it if you try. Yeah, some of this generation is millionaires. It's hard for me to keep decent clothes to wear."

Produced by WILLIE DIXON

OTIS RUSH

1956-1958

Cobra

RECORDINGS

Featuring: Willie Dixon, Shakey Horton, Little Walter, Lafayette Leake, Matt Murphy, and Ike Turner

Original recordings of "I Can't Quit You Baby", "All Your Love", and "Double Trouble".

BUDDY GUY

For most of his career, Buddy Guy was the world's greatest, best-known, unknown guitarist. He was the best known because his name was mentioned every time Eric Clapton or Keith Richards gave an interview. He was the greatest because Clapton said he was, so millions of people believed it even though they had never heard him play. He was unknown because his reputation was based almost entirely on live performances. Everyone agreed that you couldn't prove Buddy Guy's genius by listening to his records. He hadn't even made one in more than a decade.

Guy's smash 1991 CD, "Damn Right I've Got the Blues," changed all that. It sold more than six hundred thousand copies worldwide, modest by Pearl Jam standards but huge for a blues record. Both "Damn Right" and its successor, "Feels Like Rain," won Grammys. Buddy

A Buddy Guy concert performance in 1966, sharing the bill with Otis Rush and Little Walter.

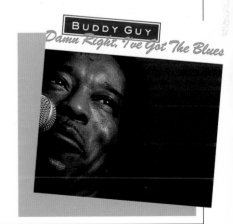

A Buddy Guy concert performance in 1966, sharing the bill with Otis Rush and Little Walter.

Guy is even starting to receive lifetime achievement awards.

But he is not ready to retire. Buddy Guy still has a few more things to do, and he is a decade younger than B. B. King, and almost two behind John Lee Hooker.

Guy's age is significant (he was born in 1936) because he is closer to the rock-and-roll generation than to the era of King, Hooker, and Muddy Waters. Even Chuck Berry and Bo Diddley are nearer King's age than Guy's. Bill Wyman, the former bass player for the Rolling Stones, is the same age as Guy. John Mayall is three years older. Clapton, Richards, Jimmy Page, Jeff Beck, Peter Green, Mick Jagger, Steve Winwood, Carlos Santana, Jimi Hendrix, and many other rock artists of their generation who cite Guy as an influence are just six to ten years his juniors.

That difference in ages partly explains Buddy Guy's influence and appeal. In the early 1960s, when most of today's rock legends were in their late teens and early twenties, just starting to chase rock-and-roll dreams, Buddy Guy was in his mid-twenties and the lead guitarist in the Muddy Waters band. What could be cooler than that? Waters was the master, but he was almost fifty. Guy was young and doing the hot, new thing: playing guitar fast and wild behind Waters, Little Walter, Howlin' Wolf, and Koko Taylor. Eric Clapton and Jeff Beck were particularly enamored of Guy's playing on some tracks cut at the Copacabana in Chicago in 1963, a recording date that featured both Waters and Wolf.

Soon Clapton, Hendrix, and all the rest were rocketing to the moon while Buddy Guy's career stayed on a lower trajectory. He said he was thrilled just to play with Waters, Wolf, Little Walter, and the rest—his idols—and in one sense that was true. He was endorsed by Muddy Waters and B. B. King, all the approval he really needed. If Waters and King said he could play, what did it matter what anyone else thought?

The people not with the program were Leonard Chess, who owned the record company, and Willie Dixon, who produced all the recording sessions. Chess and Dixon didn't like Guy's ferocious playing style or the ampli-

fier feedback and other experimental effects he was trying onstage. They definitely would not let him use them on records. They loved him as a session player, and many of these records became blues classics, but his own recordings were flat and forgettable. His last session at Chess, in 1966, yielded Koko Taylor's hit, "Wang Dang Doodle." Guy wasn't happy with the situation and, even worse, he wasn't selling. He was driving a tow truck to make ends meet.

Still, George "Buddy" Guy had come a long way from Lettsworth, Louisiana, a tiny river town near the Mississippi border. As sharecroppers, Sam and Isabell Guy and their five children made a modest living from the cotton they grew, but Isabell also cooked for the plantation owners, and Sam

worked on the railroad or cut timber. They wanted a better life for their children. For Buddy Guy ("Buddy" was a childhood nickname) and his younger brother, Phil, music was their way out.

On the family phonograph, the Guy brothers listened to the music of Lonnie Johnson, Arthur Crudup, Muddy Waters, Howlin' Wolf, Little Walter, and Lightnin' Hopkins. Buddy would play air guitar with a broom and later made his own instruments from screen wire, paint cans, and bits of wood. When he was older, he got a real guitar and played in local roadhouses. A big influence on Guy at this time was Eddie "Guitar Slim" Jones, a local celebrity with a hit record, a wild wardrobe, and an even wilder act. Jones would enter the theater on the shoulders of his "valet,"

wearing a brilliant monochrome suit and trailing several hundred feet of guitar cord behind him (in those days, there were no wireless pickups). He played a beat-up Fender Stratocaster that he abused even more during each performance.

When Buddy Guy got to Chicago in 1957 and sized up his competition, he knew he needed something extra to get noticed. He remembered Guitar Slim's onstage antics and worked them into his act. Something as simple as standing up was pretty radical in those days, when most blues guitarists played from chairs. For Buddy Guy, standing up was only the beginning. He would throw his guitar, walk on it, or hang it from the rafters. He plugged in a long cord and wandered into the crowd, out the door, and onto the street, playing all the while. His timing was always a little off anyway, so it didn't matter if he couldn't hear the band.

Onstage, Guy's strikingly handsome face always bore a wide, toothy grin. He had long, slicked-back hair and a tall, thin physique that was perfect for the loud, colorful suits he wore. He certainly looked like a young rhythm-and-blues star, like Chuck Berry or Little Richard.

But he couldn't be a star without a hit record, and Guy didn't have one. He first recorded for Cobra but that went nowhere. Then he was at Chess for seven years, and after that, Vanguard. Nothing took. Considering this lack of recording success, his touring credits are amazing. With harp player Junior Wells, he worked most of the big folk and blues festivals in the late sixties, and prime rock venues like Fillmore West. In Chicago, they played the North Side clubs that catered to young whites as well as the South Side and West Side clubs, where the audiences were mostly black. They were also popular in Europe, especially England. In 1970, they toured Europe with the Rolling Stones.

Eric Clapton persuaded Atlantic Records to give Guy a shot in 1970, but they insisted Clapton produce the album. Then in one of the worst periods of his heroin addiction, Clapton was not up to the task. Nothing went right with the record, and it wasn't even released until two years later (on Rhino as "Buddy Guy and Junior Wells Play the Blues").

After almost fifteen years of butting his head against the recording-studio wall, Buddy Guy gave up. Instead, he bought his own nightclub, the Checkerboard Lounge on the South Side of Chicago. Members of the Stones and Led Zeppelin came by and jammed whenever they were in town, which always brought notoriety for a few days. The rest of the time, it was hard work and not especially rewarding. The club was supposed to let him spend more time at home with his wife and six children. Instead, it forced him to tour to make enough money to keep both the club and the family going. The strain on his marriage was too great, and the Guys divorced in 1975.

Through the rest of the 1970s and into the 1980s, Guy continued to own the club and tour. He played in good venues, but they weren't arenas. He didn't have a record contract. In the early 1980s, he added two more names to his list of famous friends, Robert Cray and Stevie Ray Vaughn. In 1985, he sold the Checkerboard and went back to touring full-time. In 1986, Eric Clapton uttered his famous statement that "Buddy Guy is by far and without a doubt the best guitar player alive."

Guy went back into the blues-club business in 1989 when he opened Buddy Guy's Legends, a large restaurant and club located just south of the Loop in downtown Chicago. The new club had its ups and downs for the first three years, and was helped along by visits from famous friends like Clapton, the Stones, Vaughn and his brother Jimmie, David Bowie, Adrian Belew, Joe Perry, Roger Daltrey, Belinda Carlisle, and Sinead O'Connor. In 1991, Buddy Guy got the one thing that had eluded him for so long: a hit record. The record company simply let him be himself, and the success speaks for itself. He even got a video on MTV ("Mustang Sally," costarring Jeff Beck).

Buddy Guy is still not a household name, but the change since 1991 has been very satisfying for the veteran bluesman. His friends came through for him again. The guests on "Damn Right" include Clapton, Beck, and Mark Knopfler of Dire Straits. Many other blues stars have benefited from having rock-star pals—B. B. King and John Lee Hooker are the most notable examples—but it is hard to think of another musician in any idiom who has so many hardcore fans among the music world's elite. Through these relationships, Buddy Guy, even more than Muddy Waters, has been the direct link between blues and rock, a connection he has continued to revitalize throughout his career.

RECOMMENDED LISTENING

I f you are interested in listening to more of the artists featured in this book, here are some recommendations. All of these titles should be readily available on compact disc. Some are re-issues of collections previously released on vinyl, others are new compilations or, in the case of some living artists, new recordings. This is a list designed for listeners, and relatively new fans at that, not for collectors or hard-core enthusiasts; therefore, no premium has been placed on original collections, original labels, and original packaging. I recommend greatest-hits collections without apology, and some of the import anthologies are a good bargain.

If you still own a turntable, check out used record shops. They will often have bargain-priced treasures not even available on CD. Some of these stores also stock unopened LPs they acquired when the record

companies and distributors got rid of them.

RECOMMENDATIONS, BY ARTIST

Blind Lemon Jefferson. *King of the Country Blues* (Yazoo 1069), is probably still the best collection, but be prepared for lots of scratch and pop.

Memphis Minnie. *Hoodoo Lady* is from 1933-1937 (Columbia 46775). *I Ain't No Bad Gal* (Portrait 44072) is from two 1941 sessions and includes electric guitar on some tracks.

Big Joe Williams. *Classic Delta Blues* (Milestone 545) is from two 1964 sessions. *Shake Your Boogie* (Arhoolie 315) is from an early sixties session and one ten years later.

Son House. *Father of the Delta Blues* (CBS 48867) is a recent (1992) release of a 1965 studio session. *The Oberlin College Concert* (King Bee 1001) is also

from 1965.

Arthur Crudup. *That's All Right Mama* (Bluebird 61043-2) will tell you everything you need to know.

Roosevelt Sykes. *The Story of the Blues* collection of his records from 1929-1941 is good (3542-2), as is the collection of his 1945-1960 recordings in the *Blues Encore* series (52014).

Little Brother Montgomery. *Tasty Blues* (Bluesville 1012) is pretty good. It was recorded in New Jersey in 1961. There is also a Little Brother Montgomery disc in the *Chicago-The Living Legends* series (Ace CH263).

T-Bone Walker. *The Talkin' Guitar* (52010) from the *Blues Encore* series covers the essentials.

Howlin' Wolf. The three-disk Chess Box Set (MCA 3-9332) is the big ticket route. *The Best of Howlin' Wolf* (TSD-3500) from the *Masters of the Blues* series is a smaller but satisfying bite.

Robert Johnson. Go straight for the two-disk *The Complete Recordings* (Columbia 46222). It's the only Robert Johnson record you will ever need.

Lightning Hopkins. *Mojo Hand* is the two-disk Rhino anthology (Rhino 71226) and gives a good overview of his immense output.

Muddy Waters. The three-disk Chess Box Set (MCA 6-80002) is the definitive collection. *The Best of Muddy Waters* (CHD-31268) is a collection of twelve classics from 1948-1954. Also fun is the Library of Congress recording from 1941-42, now available as *The Complete Plantation Recordings* (CHD-9344).

Memphis Slim. His collection in the Chess *The Real Folk Blues* series (CHD-9270) is from 1950-1952. *Memphis Blues, The Paris Sessions* (Stash CD-11) lets you hear what he did in Europe for the second half of his career.

John Lee Hooker. *On Vee-Jay 1955-1958* (Vee Jay 713) has most of his best old stuff, with back-up from Jimmy Reed and Eddie Taylor as a bonus. *Chill Out* (Pointblank 40107) from 1995 is good recent stuff, with Carlos Santana as a bonus.

Jimmy Reed. *The Best of Jimmy Reed* (GNP/Crescendo 2-0006) is exactly that.

B. B. King. *My Sweet Little Angel* (Flair V2-39103) is good for mid-to-late 1950s sides. *Live at Cook County Jail* (MCA 31080) from 1971 was his first big crossover album. *Blues Summit* (MCA 10710) from 1993 is a duets record with a host of famous guests.

Little Walter. *The Best of Little Walter* (CHD-9192) is the best. A second volume (CHD-9292) is also available.

Freddie King. *Hideaway: The Best of Freddy King* (Rhino 71510) does the trick.

Otis Rush. The 1956-1958 Cobra Recordings (PCD01) are the must-have collection. His 1994 *Ain't Enough Coming In* (Mercury 314 518 769-2) is also very good.

Buddy Guy. Forget the old stuff and go right for *Damn Right, I've Got The Blues* (Silvertone 1462-2-J).

RECOMMENDED READING AND REFERENCE SOURCES

Herzhaft, Gerard, *Encyclopedia of the Blues,* Fayetteville: The University of Arkansas Press, 1992.

Harris, Sheldon, *Blues Who's Who,* New York: De Capo Press, 1994.

Leadbitter, Mike, *Blues Records 1943-1966,* New York: Oak Publications, 1968.

Barlow, William, *Looking Up At Down, The Emergence of Blues Culture,* Philadelphia: Temple University Press, 1989.

Charters, Samuel, *The Country Blues,* New York: De Capo Press, 1959.

Charters, Samuel, *The Legacy of the Blues,* New York: De Capo Press, 1975.

Cantor, Louis, *Wheelin' on Beale,* New York: Pharos Books, 1992.

Dixon, Willie, *I Am The Blues, The Willie Dixon Story,* New York: De Capo Press, 1989.

Garon, Paul and Beth, *Woman With Guitar, Memphis Minnie's Blues,* New York: De Capo Press, 1992.

Lomax, Alan, *The Land Where The Blues Began,* New York: Delta, 1993.

McKee, Margaret, *Beale Black & Blue,* Baton Rouge: Louisiana State University Press, 1981.

Oliver, Paul, *Blues Fell This Morning, Meaning In The Blues,* Cambridge: Cambridge University Press, 1960.

Rowe, Mike, *Chicago Blues,* New York: De Capo Press, 1975.

Shaw, Arnold, *Honkers and Shouters, The Golden Years of Rhythm and Blues,* New York: Collier Books, 1978.

Wilcock, Donald, *Damn Right, I've Got The Blues, Buddy Guy And The Blues Roots Of Rock And Roll,* San Francisco: Woodford Press, 1993.

Guitar Player Magazine (Searchable online via Magazine Database Plus on Compuserve.)

Down Beat Magazine (Searchable online via Magazine Database Plus on Compuserve.)

All-Music Guide Database on Compuserve.